Christian Heroes: Then & Now

# COUNT ZINZENDORF

## Firstfruit

Christian Heroes: Then & Now

# COUNT ZINZENDORF

## Firstfruit

JANET & GEOFF BENGE

YWAM PUBLISHING
P.O. BOX 55787 SEATTLE, WA 98155

YWAM Publishing is the publishing ministry of Youth With A Mission (YWAM), an international missionary organization of Christians from many denominations dedicated to presenting Jesus Christ to this generation. To this end, YWAM has focused its efforts in three main areas: (1) training and equipping believers for their part in fulfilling the Great Commission (Matthew 28:19), (2) personal evangelism, and (3) mercy ministry (medical and relief work).

For a free catalog of books and materials, call (425) 771-1153 or (800) 922-2143. Visit us online at www.ywampublishing.com.

**Count Zinzendorf: Firstfruit**


Published by YWAM Publishing
a ministry of Youth With A Mission
P.O. Box 55787, Seattle, WA 98155

ISBN 978-1-57658-262-6 (paperback)
ISBN 978-1-57658-606-8 (e-book)

Library of Congress Cataloging-in-Publication Data
Benge, Janet, 1958–
Count Zinzendorf : firstfruit / Janet and Geoff Benge.
p. cm. — (Christian heroes, then & now)
ISBN 1-57658-262-0
1. Zinzendorf, Nicolaus Ludwig, Graf von, 1700–1760.
2. Moravians—Germany—Biography—Juvenile literature.
I. Benge, Geoff, 1954– . II. Title. III. Series.
BX8593.Z6B42 2005
284'.6'092—dc22
[B] 2005018875



Fifth printing 2023

Printed in the United States of America

## Christian Heroes: Then & Now

Adoniram Judson
Albert Schweitzer
Amy Carmichael
Betty Greene
Brother Andrew
Cameron Townsend
Charles Mulli
Clarence Jones
Corrie ten Boom
Count Zinzendorf
C. S. Lewis
C. T. Studd
David Bussau
David Livingstone
Dietrich Bonhoeffer
D. L. Moody
Elisabeth Elliot
Eric Liddell
Florence Young
Francis Asbury
George Müller
Gladys Aylward
Helen Roseveare
Hudson Taylor
Ida Scudder
Isobel Kuhn
Jacob DeShazer
Jim Elliot
John Flynn
John Newton
John Wesley
John Williams
Jonathan Goforth
Klaus-Dieter John
Lillian Trasher
Loren Cunningham
Lottie Moon
Mary Slessor
Mildred Cable
Nate Saint
Norman Grubb
Paul Brand
Rachel Saint
Richard Wurmbrand
Rowland Bingham
Samuel Zwemer
Sundar Singh
Wilfred Grenfell
William Booth
William Carey

*Available in paperback, e-book, and audiobook formats.Unit study curriculum guides are available for select biographies.*

*www.YWAMpublishing.com*

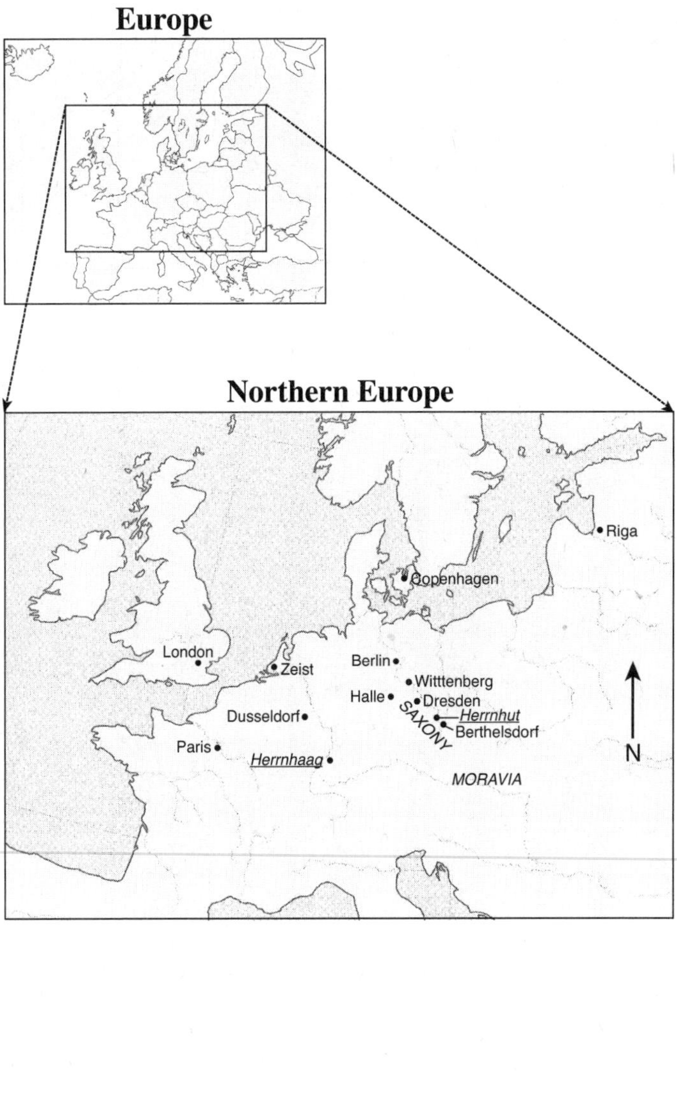

Europe
Northern Europe
Riga
Copenhagen
London
Zeist
Berlin
Witttenberg
Halle
Dresden
SAXONY
Herrnhut
Berthelsdorf
Dusseldorf
Paris
Herrnhaag
MORAVIA
N

# Contents

Chapter 1

# Disappointed but Never Deterred

They met few people out here. There were no roads, no castles, no bustling towns, just rolling green hills covered with vegetation—so different from Europe. Back in Saxony, Count Ludwig von Zinzendorf would have been riding in the luxury of a carriage. But here, deep in Indian country, he rode on horseback.

Guided by Chief Skikellimy and several braves, Ludwig and his companions wound their way up Pennsylvania's Wyoming Valley, riding steadily toward the home of the Shawnee Indians in the valley's upper reaches. As he rode, Ludwig thought of all the wonderful things that might come from this long journey. He hoped to negotiate with the

Shawnees for permission for missionaries to enter their tribal land and live and work among them.

All went well as the party made their way along the Susquehanna River—until they forded a creek. Halfway across the creek, the girth strap on Ludwig's saddle broke, and Ludwig tumbled backward from his horse into the frigid water, his saddle landing on top of him. Chief Skikellimy and the braves burst into uproarious laughter.

Martin Mack, one of Ludwig's traveling companions, rushed to Ludwig's aid, lifted the saddle from him, and pulled him to his feet.

"My poor brother," Ludwig apologized in embarrassment. "I am an endless source of trouble!"

Martin clapped Ludwig on the back. "The way is treacherous," he countered. "It could easily have happened to anyone. You stand aside, and I'll take a look at your saddle."

Once the saddle had been repaired and put back on his horse, Ludwig mounted up, and the group continued on. They traveled for several more days, stopping in the evening to pitch their tents and prepare a meal from the meager supplies they carried with them.

At last they reached a cluster of Shawnee villages. Since Ludwig imagined that it would take a number of days to win the confidence of the Shawnees, he paid closer attention than usual to where he pitched his tent. Finally he chose what seemed to be a good site, about twenty yards from his companions' tents.

All went well the first night. The following day Ludwig sat on his bedroll and spread his books and papers on the ground in front of him. He jotted down several verses of a hymn he was composing and then picked up his journal and began making an entry for the day. As he wrote, a small movement caught his eye. He ignored it. Soon a huge snake was slithering across the papers spread in front of him. Ludwig froze. What should he do? He had no idea. He dared not breathe as he waited for the snake to strike him.

The creature simply ignored Ludwig and continued across the papers, disappearing out under the side of the tent. Ludwig let out a deep breath and put down his pen. Then, without any warning, the scene repeated itself as a second snake glided over the papers and disappeared outside. As soon as the snake was gone, Ludwig leaped up and bolted from his tent. He begged several Indians to come and see where the snakes were coming from, but he did not anticipate their reaction. They checked around inside his tent and then burst into gales of laughter.

One of the Indians pointed to a hole in the ground. "You have pitched your tent over the mouth of a snake den!" he said, shaking his head in disbelief. "Either you get used to the snakes, or you'll have to move."

Ludwig felt himself turning red with embarrassment. Back in Saxony no one ever laughed at him. They wouldn't have dared! Besides, he seldom made mistakes like this. In Saxony he owned a castle and did not have to worry about scratching around for a good site to pitch a tent! Despite his humiliation, Count Zinzendorf was undeterred. He had come on a mission to negotiate with the Shawnees, and that was what he was going to do.

As Ludwig began to talk with the Shawnee chiefs, it soon became obvious that his negotiations were going nowhere. The Shawnees did not trust him, no matter how hard he tried to convince them that he had come in peace as a friend. Ludwig also noticed that Chief Skikellimy and the braves with him were growing suspicious of the Shawnees' intentions.

Deeply frustrated by the situation, Ludwig sat in his tent one night and poured out his heart to God in prayer, asking Him what he should do. The next day Conrad Weiser, a man Ludwig had befriended in the colony, arrived at the Shawnee village. He was a well-known mediator and interpreter between Indians and whites. He was also well respected by the Shawnees, and he was able to quickly size up the situation.

That evening Conrad and Ludwig sat by the fire and talked.

"You were in great danger, Count Zinzendorf," Conrad began. "The Shawnees were preparing to kill you all."

Ludwig's mouth dropped open. "Why?" he stammered. "I have done them no harm."

"The Shawnees believed that you were an agent of people who want to get their hands on the silver deposits located in their territory. So they had decided the best thing for them to do was kill you all as a message to others who might come seeking their silver. I managed to convince them that you have no such intentions—that you have no interest in their silver, just their souls."

"You are an answer to prayer then, my friend!" Ludwig exclaimed.

"Perhaps," Conrad replied, "but I am afraid I have been unable to change the Shawnees' minds regarding your request to send missionaries among them. On that they steadfastly refuse."

"What are we to do then?" Ludwig asked.

"Ah," Conrad said, "perhaps time will change things."

"And prayer," Ludwig added.

The following day the party packed up, and Conrad led them back the way they had come. As they rode along, Ludwig was disappointed that things had not gone as well with the Shawnees as he had hoped, but his zeal was not dampened. He believed that in time the Shawnees would have a change of heart and invite missionaries to come and live among them and teach them.

As the narrow trail led them back alongside the Susquehanna River, Ludwig thought back to his privileged life in Saxony. If his grandmother could see him now, in his muddy buckskins, with uncombed hair, and with only a few meager rations in his knapsack! She had preened and prepared him for life in the royal court in Dresden. But here he was, laying aside all that ease and privilege to be the first European nobleman to leave behind the edges of North American civilization and travel deep into Indian country. His life had certainly taken many unexpected detours from the course that was mapped out for him growing up in Saxony.

Chapter 2

# "This Shame Shall Not Crush Me"

Four-year-old Nicolaus Ludwig von Zinzendorf wanted to scream, but he fought back the impulse. He also wanted to wave after the coach as it rumbled down the road, but he did not want to send the wrong message—that it was all right for his mother to leave without him. How could she? Why couldn't she take him with her? And why did he now have to stay with his grandmother? Nobody had bothered to ask him what *he* wanted!

All these thoughts and emotions coursed through him as he watched the coachman crack the whip. The carriage sped up and soon disappeared into the surrounding woods. Ludwig stood and stared, the tears rolling down his cheeks. His mother was leaving him behind to live with her new husband, fifty-year-old Field Marshall von Natzmer, in Berlin. Now Ludwig would have to live with his grandmother and his aunt and uncle at Gross-Hennersdorf castle in Upper Lusatia, sixty miles east of Dresden. He had never known his father, who had died of tuberculosis when Ludwig was six weeks old, and his mother was now leaving him behind too. He had no idea whether he would ever see her again.

Just when Ludwig thought he could no longer stand the pain, he felt his grandmother wrap her arm around him. "Come, Ludwig. Things will work out. I will take care of you, and God will take care of you. You will see." With that she guided him inside the castle.

Baroness Henriette Katrina von Gersdorf was true to her word. She took good care of her grandson, who soon was studying under the guidance of a watchful tutor. Ludwig's life quickly fell into a busy routine, and it wasn't long before the boy stopped thinking about his mother all of the time.

In the morning Ludwig had breakfast with his grandmother and then went off to reading class with his tutor. He ate lunch with his mother's younger sister and brother, Aunt Henriette and Uncle Nicolaus. After more studies in the afternoon with his tutor, Ludwig sat down to dinner in the castle's ornate dining room with his grandmother, aunt, and uncle.

During dinner the baroness would quiz her grandson on what he had learned that day. Ludwig knew how much she wanted him to do well in his studies. Unlike most noblewomen of her day, the countess had a well-rounded education herself. She was an accomplished oil painter, was fluent in Greek and Latin, and had a special interest in theology.

Indeed, the part of Ludwig's education that his grandmother and aunt cared about most was his spiritual upbringing. Both the Gersdorf and Zinzendorf families were strong Lutherans. They went to church several times a week and sang hymns and had Bible readings every day in their castle. Baroness von Gersdorf encouraged Ludwig to write his own hymns and poems. She also often reminded Ludwig that his godfather had been Philip Jacob Spener, the great leader of Pietism in Germany. As well, August Franke, another leader of Pietism, often stayed at the castle and took a special interest in praying with Ludwig.

In fact, just about every person Ludwig knew was a strong Christian. So it was not surprising that he grew up thinking that every young boy prayed, sang hymns, and read his Bible. Ludwig had a simple, trusting faith in God. He would often write down his prayers on small pieces of paper, which he then threw from one of the upstairs windows, scattering them to the wind for God to read. And he had no reason to believe that God did not read his prayers and answer them all.

It was Ludwig's devotion to prayer and Bible reading that kept the castle from being ransacked one day in 1706. Six-year-old Ludwig was sitting at the table with his Bible open, reading and praying, as he did each day, when the door to Gross-Hennersdorf castle burst open and a detachment of Swedish soldiers stormed in. The Swedes had overrun Saxony, the small German kingdom where Ludwig lived, and the soldiers were going through the countryside, rounding up supplies from various estates. Ludwig looked up when the soldiers burst in and then returned to his prayer and Bible reading. The soldiers stopped in their tracks and stared. Ludwig kept right on praying, and after a few moments the soldiers turned and left.

Two minutes later Baroness von Gersdorf and Aunt Henriette came running into the room. "Ludwig! Ludwig! We are safe. What did you say to the soldiers?" his grandmother gasped. "They left the castle saying they could not ransack this place because God watched over it."

Ludwig was puzzled. "I just kept reading my Bible and praying," he replied.

His grandmother tousled his brown hair. "Were you a little afraid?" she asked.

"No, Grandmother," Ludwig replied. "I was reading how even the wind and waves obey Jesus, and it made me feel safe."

"Quite right," his grandmother agreed. "God can keep us safe from harm. We shall have to tell your mother all about it when she comes next week."

"My mother is coming?" Ludwig asked, overcome with excitement.

"Yes," the countess replied. "I was just coming to tell you when the soldiers arrived. She sent me a letter. Fredrick and Susanne are coming too."

Young Ludwig's heart raced. Fredrick and Susanne were his older half-brother and half-sister from his father's first marriage. Ludwig was the only child of his father's second marriage. When their father had died, the two older children had gone to live with their Uncle Otto von Zinzendorf, while Ludwig had stayed with his mother until she remarried.

Now that he was living with his grandmother, Ludwig always looked forward to seeing his mother. He thoroughly enjoyed her visits, including this one, and he continued to enjoy her visits in the coming years—until the time she sent word that she was coming to take him away. That time ten-year-old Ludwig dreaded her arrival. His mother and his grandmother had both decided that he should attend a boarding school in the city of Halle, 120 miles away. Although the two women agreed that this would be a good place for Ludwig to go to school, Uncle Otto, who controlled the Zinzendorf family money, was not happy with the decision. To him Halle was a hotbed of Pietists, Christians who put great emphasis on people's knowing and experiencing God in their hearts. Uncle Otto wanted to send Ludwig to a more traditional Lutheran school that emphasized finding God in the traditions and theology of the church. Eventually, though, Ludwig's mother and grandmother won Uncle Otto over, and he agreed to pay for Ludwig's education in Halle. So, on August 5, 1710, Ludwig's mother bundled him up and took him away from his grandmother's castle.

As the coach carrying him, his mother, and his tutor, Christian Hohmann, bounced along through the Saxon countryside toward Halle, Ludwig was lost in his thoughts, wondering what to expect when he arrived at his destination. Eventually his mother's words broke through his musing.

"I am sure you will enjoy living in Halle. There are so many interesting things to see there. Professor Franke does much more besides run the Paedagogium, the school you will be attending."

"What else does he do?" Ludwig asked.

"He runs a large orphanage, a school for poor boys and girls, and a print shop that produces Bibles. There's even a botanical garden and a drug store. I am sure you will find many things to interest you," his mother said. "Living in the country with your grandmother has no doubt been fun, but now it is time to experience city life. After all, when you grow up, you will be serving in the royal court at Dresden, like your father did."

Ludwig did not share his mother's enthusiasm. All he knew was that he was leaving behind his grandmother and Aunt Henriette and the warm, Christian atmosphere they had created, where arguments were solved with prayer and forgiveness. He tried to comfort himself with the thought that Professor August Franke's school was a Christian school. His hope was that his life there would be as pleasant as it had been at his grandmother's castle.

Finally the wheels of the coach crackled along the cobblestone streets of Halle. Ludwig looked out the window at this town that was to be his new home. It was grim compared to Gross-Hennersdorf. The buildings that lined the streets were close together, people were everywhere, and barely a tree was in sight. Gone were the woods and meadows he liked to wander in around the castle. To make matters worse, a steady rain had set in, making everything seem dank and heavy. Eventually the coach pulled to a halt in front of a large, gray, stone building. A servant helped Ludwig and his mother down from the coach and led them inside, where Professor Franke awaited them in the foyer.

"Countess von Natzmer, so wonderful to see you," the professor said politely.

Ludwig's mother curtsied. "Thank you, Herr Franke. This is my son, Count Nicolaus Ludwig von Zinzendorf. You have met him before at my mother's castle."

August Franke gave a small bow and then shook Ludwig's hand. "It is a pleasure to meet you again. I will do everything I can to make sure you are comfortable."

"It is good to make your acquaintance again, Herr Franke," Ludwig said respectfully.

"And here is Ludwig's tutor, Herr Christian Hohmann. He is particularly gifted in teaching Latin and French, and I am sure you will find him most useful," the countess said.

Ludwig watched as his tutor bowed to Professor Franke. His mother had told him that it was normal for the sons of nobility to bring their own tutors with them to boarding school. Christian Hohmann would help teach all of the boys at the school, but he would room with Ludwig and keep a close eye on his studies.

"I must be going soon," Ludwig's mother said. "It is not good for the boy if I dally here. However, before I go, I must tell you one thing. My son is a sharp and intelligent young man, but he must be reined in lest he become proud and presume too much on his abilities."

Professor Franke nodded, and Ludwig felt himself turning bright red at his mother's remarks. He became even more embarrassed when he realized that two older boys standing nearby had heard her words. The two boys smirked at each other.

Much to Ludwig's chagrin, word of what his mother had told Professor Franke spread quickly around the school. Soon the other boys began to taunt him. "There goes the boy who is too smart for his own good!" they laughed. "Better watch out for him. He has pride written all over him."

Everywhere Ludwig went, students seemed to be whispering and nudging each other as he passed by. On several occasions boys tripped him in the corridors, and his books sprawled across the marble floors. He picked them up as quickly as he could and hurried off to class, but he was late twice. The teacher would not listen to his explanation, and Ludwig felt the sting of a paddle across his backside. Another time a student tipped pepper into his soup, and when Ludwig coughed and spluttered over it, he was made to stand outside the dining hall for the remainder of the lunchtime.

For the first time, Ludwig realized just how small and puny he was. At home in the castle, it had not mattered that he was short and that his lungs ached when he exercised, but at school he was constantly picked on because of his size.

All of this was a rude awakening for a ten-year-old boy who was used to being loved and accepted by everyone who knew him. Not surprisingly, it was only a matter of weeks before Ludwig was dreading to get out of bed in the morning. His tutor was unwilling to do anything about the situation. In fact, he seemed to make things worse. When Ludwig complained to him about the way the bigger boys were picking on him, Christian replied, "You deserve the treatment you get. Your beloved grandmother can't protect you here! It's time to toughen up and stop acting like a spoiled brat."

Ludwig felt tears forming in his eyes, but Herr Hohmann had not finished with him yet. "I've always thought that your grandmother thought far too much of you, and if you tell her I said that, I shall tell her you are too lazy to study."

Ludwig was horrified. Where could he go to get help? What if the older boys carried through on their threats to beat him up? Who would believe it wasn't his fault? He had no answers to these questions.

Professor Franke was certainly not the man to go to. He believed Christian's lies about Ludwig being lazy. At lunch the boys ate with the professor. They sat in order of social rank, and being a count of the Holy Roman Empire, the highest rank of counts in German nobility, Ludwig sat right next to Professor Franke. But this honored position brought him no comfort. Throughout the meal the professor would chastise Ludwig, taking pains to point out all of the things the boy did not yet know. Sometimes, to make his point, he would order Ludwig to stand in the street with donkey's ears on his head and a placard around his neck that read "Lazy Donkey."

Ludwig lived in a state of fear and shock. The atmosphere of the Paedagogium, despite its being a Christian school, was very different from his grandmother's castle. It felt to him more like hell than heaven on earth. Despite his cruel treatment, Ludwig refused to let the situation defeat him. As he lay in bed at night anguishing over the unjust treatment that had been meted out to him during the day, he would mutter over and over to himself in Latin, "This shame shall not crush me. On the contrary, it shall raise me up."

Chapter 3

# Order of the Grain of Mustard Seed

After Ludwig had endured the bullying by the other boys for nearly two years, it gradually began to die down. School life slowly improved for him, though he was often homesick and friendless. In 1712 Christian left, and another tutor, Daniel Cristenius, replaced him. Daniel was a gifted scholar and good teacher, but he had little respect for the views of Pietists and seemed to take his frustrations with these views out on Ludwig. Herr Cristenius taunted Ludwig when he tried to pray or read his Bible, but Ludwig continued anyway. Ludwig also sought out friends among the few boys who were not bullies. Under his urging this handful of the less popular boys started small prayer meetings. Whenever and wherever they could get away from the ridicule of the other boys and the mocking eyes of Daniel, they met together and prayed fervently.

One particular lunchtime in 1712, Ludwig sat at his usual dining place beside Professor Franke. Across the table from him sat a man who was visiting the professor.

"Allow me to introduce you to Bartholomaus Ziegenbalg," Professor Franke said to the boys as lunch was served. "Herr Ziegenbalg is a graduate of Halle University and now a missionary with the Danish-Halle mission in India."

Ludwig's ears pricked up at this last comment. A missionary! He had never before seen a real live missionary who served in a foreign land. As soon as the meal was served, Ludwig introduced himself to Bartholomaus. "Please tell me all about your missionary work," he requested politely.

At first Bartholomaus looked a little surprised that a twelve-year-old boy would be interested in what he did, but he soon warmed to his topic.

"I, with my associate Heinrich Plütschau, have been working in Tranquebar on the southeast coast of India. India is very different from Europe. The language, the food, the people, the weather—everything is so different. Slowly but steadily the Tamil people are responding to the message of salvation."

Bartholomaus took a breath, and Ludwig leaned forward in his seat, eager to hear more.

"But we have had our share of setbacks. The Danish East India Company is very suspicious of our work. They would rather we let the people alone and went home, and they have made things difficult for us. They have even thrown me in prison. But we progress. The church there is growing, and we have translated the New Testament into the local language."

"So you are fluent in the local dialect? Is it called Tamil?" Ludwig asked.

"Yes. Tamil is a very different language from those of Europe, but I have managed to learn it." With that Bartholomaus spoke a few sentences in Tamil.

Ludwig was most impressed. And he was surprised when someone in the room answered back in Tamil. Ludwig's eyes followed in the direction of the voice, and there on the other side of the dining room sat an Indian man. Ludwig had been so focused on the conversation with Bartholomaus that he had not noticed the man. Now he stared at the first non-European he had ever seen. The man was of medium build, was dressed in white, and had skin and hair as dark as coal. Ludwig could not divert his gaze from him.

"He is one of our early converts and is now a great help in our work," Bartholomaus said, following Ludwig's gaze.

Ludwig sat spellbound through lunch, listening to all Bartholomaus had to say about being a missionary in India. When lunch was over, he could hardly wait to catch up with his Swiss friend Frederick von Watteville.

"Frederick, I had the most amazing conversation over lunch with Bartholomaus Ziegenbalg. He has such interesting stories to tell about life there. And did you see the Indian man he brought with him?"

Frederick nodded, and Ludwig went on to tell him all that he had learned.

"I am going to make a vow today," Frederick said very seriously when Ludwig had finished speaking, "I am going to vow to do all I can do to work toward the conversion of the heathen."

Ludwig nodded in agreement. "I will join you. Perhaps we can do more together than either of us could do alone."

"I am sure we could," Frederick agreed, clapping Ludwig on the back. "Though, of course, it would be out of the question for either of us to be missionaries. Think of what our families would say!"

Ludwig nodded glumly. Even though he had been raised by a pious grandmother, his future was all mapped out for him. He, like Frederick, was the son of a noble family. When he finished school, he would go on to university and then take a position in the royal court of Saxony. Frederick would follow the same course in Switzerland.

"Although we cannot go, we can seek out others who will go and help them to be successful," Frederick said.

"Yes, we could!" Ludwig replied, thinking of some of the ways he would be able to smooth the way for missionaries when he got older. "We must remind each other of this pledge and keep each other to it."

When Frederick and Ludwig told their other friends, Anton Walbaum, Georg von Söhlenthal, and Johannes von Jony, about their vow, the other boys got very excited. Ludwig saw an opportunity and quickly formed the five of them into a fraternity. The boys were the core of what would become known as the "Order of the Grain of Mustard Seed." Ludwig chose this name after a passage in the Bible in which Jesus talks about a mustard seed being the smallest of seeds but growing into the biggest of trees. The name seemed fitting, since they were only twelve- and thirteen-year-old boys with big dreams of sending out many missionaries around the world.

In June 1713 Ludwig was not well and returned to Gross-Hennersdorf castle. He had a weak chest and was prone to lung problems. Baroness von Gersdorf was concerned about him, especially since both Ludwig's father and grandfather had died in their late thirties, and they had lived longer than most Zinzendorf men.

While he recuperated, Ludwig continued with his studies under the guidance of his tutor. Finally, in September, he was well enough to return to school in Halle, though he was less than enthusiastic about going back. It had been so easy to again be in the warm and encouraging environment of his grandmother's castle.

Back at the Paedagogium, Ludwig did well at his studies. He was soon reading the New Testament in Greek and enjoyed the Greek classics as well. He also loved Latin and spoke French as fluently as he spoke his native German. In addition, he found poetry a joy and composed many poems, some of them containing up to three hundred verses. By the time their final year at the Paedagogium rolled around, Ludwig and his friend Johannes had finished all their classes. Since they were too young to go on to university, a special class was set up for them to study science, philosophy, and theology.

Finally his days at the Paedagogium were over, and Ludwig left Halle in April 1716, confident he would be back in the fall to begin university. But this was not to be. When he arrived at his grandmother's castle, Ludwig learned that his Uncle Otto had enrolled him at the University of Wittenberg. To his uncle, Halle University was too Prussian. The University of Wittenberg, on the other hand, was Saxon and the only place fit to prepare a young man who was destined for a life in the service of the king of Saxony.

Ludwig was disappointed at his uncle's decision, but he knew better than to complain about it. To his surprise, when he told his grandmother about the University of Wittenberg, she agreed with the change. "It is time you fit your education to your social rank," she told him. "Within a few years you will be secretary of state, as your father was, and you must know how to conduct yourself and the affairs of state properly."

Ludwig spent the summer at Gross-Hennersdorf reading books from the baroness's library, riding in the countryside, writing poems, listening to lectures by his tutor, and taking long walks with his Aunt Henriette.

Summer drew to a close, and the time to start university approached. Ludwig and his tutor, Daniel, visited Ludwig's Uncle Otto, who gave Ludwig firm written instructions as to how he was to behave while at Wittenberg. Ludwig's uncle also laid out the things he expected his nephew to learn while at university. Among other things, Ludwig was to exercise regularly and take lessons in dancing and fencing. He was to sleep regular hours and attend public worship rather than conventicles, private religious meetings. The message was clear. Ludwig was to keep himself busy, learn how to act like a count, and avoid participating in religious behavior outside the Lutheran Church. Ludwig was glad that Uncle Otto did not know about the Order of the Grain of Mustard Seed. That knowledge would undoubtedly have sent his uncle into a rage.

In August 1716 Ludwig and Daniel, who was employed to make sure that Uncle Otto's instructions were followed, set out for Wittenberg. They arrived on August 25. It was Ludwig's first trip to the city, and he peered out the window of the coach to see this place that had had such an impact on the course of Christianity in Europe.

The coach passed the castle church, the great medieval stone church that had been the birthplace of Protestantism. It was here that a Saxon priest named Martin Luther, then a professor at Wittenberg

University, had nailed to the church door his ninety-five theses challenging certain practices and doctrines of the Catholic Church. While this act began as an effort to reform the Catholic Church, it eventually led to the forming of the Lutheran Church and other Protestant denominations throughout Europe. Ludwig eyed the church with awe. In several weeks Wittenberg would be celebrating the two hundredth anniversary of Martin Luther's bold act, and people were busy cleaning and tidying the church building and grounds for the occasion.

Ludwig finally arrived at the university and was shown to his new lodgings. He was to stay in the home of Burgomaster Keil, where he had his own private drawing room and a combination study and bedroom. He also had a servant to attend to his needs. It was all very elegant, befitting someone of Ludwig's social rank. To add a personal touch to his new accommodation, Ludwig brought along with him a number of gilt-framed portraits, including those of the kings of Prussia and Poland, the Russian czar, his grandfather von Gersdorf, and his great grandfather. Once the servant had hung the pictures on the walls of the drawing room and study, Ludwig felt quite at home.

Soon Ludwig was busy following the directives his uncle had laid out for him, though he still found time to write letters in German, French, Greek, and Latin. He studied philosophy, church law, feudal law, and languages, but he found Hebrew a struggle. He also disliked mathematics. Uncle Otto had forbidden him to take any theology classes because they would only encourage his strange "preoccupation with religion," as he put it. However, whenever he could, Ludwig read theology books and studied his Bible in Greek.

In addition to keeping up with his classroom studies, Ludwig played badminton, chess, and balloon, a soccerlike game played with a large, inflated leather ball. He also took classes in fencing and dancing, as his uncle had instructed, but he did not particularly enjoy either of these activities, since he did not believe in fighting or see any value in dancing. He viewed these activities simply as items to be checked off in the quest to fulfill all his uncle's requirements.

Ludwig made the time to spend two hours each day in prayer and meditation. Somehow he also kept in touch with his old friends from the Paedagogium in Halle. As the five young men wrote to one another, the Order of the Grain of Mustard Seed continued to take shape. The members of the order pledged to stay true to the teachings of Jesus, show love and kindness to their fellow men, avoid gambling, look out for the welfare of others at all times, and work for the conversion of others. Ludwig had rings made that were inscribed with the words, "No one liveth unto himself." He sent one to each member of the order, along with a green silk ribbon embroidered with a cross and a mustard tree.

In Wittenberg, Ludwig found himself at the center of the struggle taking place within the Lutheran

Church between Pietists and Traditionalists, who emphasized strict observance of Lutheran practice and theology. Since Halle was the center of the Pietist movement and Wittenberg, home of the Traditionalists, Ludwig had a good grasp of both sides of the struggle. He hated to see the way in which gossip and misinformation were keeping the two sides from really understanding each other's point of view.

Ludwig wrote a tract titled *Various Thoughts on Peace to the Quarreling Lutheran Churches,* which was well received. Soon he found himself trying to arrange a meeting between August Franke and Professor Wernsdorf, theology professor at Wittenberg, in the hope of settling the dispute once and for all. It was a bold step for an eighteen-year-old, but something inside Ludwig drove him on. He hated to see Christian men arguing over religious matters.

When Ludwig's mother heard about his efforts, she was horrified. Soon afterward Ludwig received a letter from his stepfather, Field Marshall von Natzmer, forbidding him from having anything more to do with trying to heal the rift within the Lutheran Church. It was ridiculous, his stepfather wrote, to imagine that an eighteen-year-old boy would think he could do anything about such a difficult problem. From now on Ludwig was to remember that he was a count, and counts did not meddle in church affairs. Church affairs were left to clergymen.

Ludwig had no choice but to obey his stepfather, especially with his tutor, Daniel, watching his every move and sending regular reports home. Disappointed that he had not been able to do what he set out to do, Ludwig withdrew from trying to arrange a meeting between the two men. Instead he poured his efforts into his studies, and soon he was finished at Wittenberg University. Upon graduation Ludwig did what every wealthy student of the day did. He took a year off to tour Europe and round out his education.

Chapter 4

# Ecce Homo

Ludwig climbed the stone steps of the art gallery in Düsseldorf. The doorman bowed low, and Ludwig nodded in recognition of the gesture. It was May 20, 1719, and this was the fifth art gallery he had been to since setting out on the trip a week before. Ludwig strolled around, taking in the various masterpieces that were on display. With him were his new tutor, Herr Riederer, and his older half-brother, Fredrick, who had joined him for the early portion of the grand tour of Europe. The excursion to the art gallery was much like the others Ludwig had made on the trip, until he came to one particular painting. For some reason he felt attracted to it. He stopped and studied it closely. The painting, by Domenico Feti, was titled *Ecce Homo (Behold the Man)*, and it showed Jesus with a crown of thorns on His head. At the bottom of the picture, the artist had painted the words:

This I have done for you.
What have you done for me?

The question astonished Ludwig. It seemed to hang in the air as he pondered what, indeed, he had done for Christ. The usual answers came to mind. He had loved Him, read the Bible, prayed, and sang hymns, but somehow these things seemed insignificant compared to all that Christ had done by dying on the cross. Ludwig repeated the question to himself: *What have you done for me?* His mind went back to the dining room at the Paedagogium in Halle. He thought about the time he sat at the table listening to all that Bartholomaus Ziegenbalg, the missionary from India, had to say. Now, there was a man who was doing something for Christ!

"I will do more," Ludwig vowed quietly as he stood in front of the painting. "My life will not be spent in idle touring and visiting."

"Don't you want to see the rest of the gallery?" Fredrick asked, his voice breaking into Ludwig's thoughts. "You've been standing here in a trance for fifteen minutes."

"Oh, yes, I suppose I must go on," Ludwig replied, taking one last look at the painting.

Ludwig went on to view the work of famous Dutch and German artists, but he could not get out of his mind the idea that it was time to do something for Christ.

The grand tour continued on through Leipzig, Eisenach, Frankfurt am Main, and Mainz and then to Utrecht in the Netherlands, where Fredrick said good-bye and returned home. Ludwig then enrolled in a three-month course at the University of Utrecht, where he studied theology and medicine. Despite all he had seen and learned so far, nothing impressed or challenged him like the *Ecce Homo* painting.

Everywhere he went, nineteen-year-old Count Ludwig von Zinzendorf was invited into the highest orders of society. In Amsterdam he dined with the Prince of Orange, rode in the country with other counts, and visited still more nobles. But all of this was somewhat boring to Ludwig. What really was exciting to him was meeting with bishops and common people from every branch of Christianity. He talked with members of the Reformed Church, Roman Catholic cardinals, Lutherans, Mennonites, Armenians, Anglicans, mystics, and Pietists in every place he visited. And the more he talked to these people with their different views of religion, the more convinced he became that they would all find that they had much in common if they could just stop and listen to one another.

As he traveled around, two thoughts—*What have you done for me?* and *All Christian religions have a common bond*—whirled around in Ludwig's head until they merged into one big idea. Right there in the middle of a lavish tour of Europe, Ludwig caught a vision of his life's work. What could he do for Christ? It was so obvious to him now: he could use his life and his money to try to bring *all* Christians together into one family—one fellowship that would accept and tolerate one another's differences.

By the time he and Herr Riederer arrived in Paris, Ludwig could think of little else. He did his duty and visited the court of the duke of Orléans, the French regent, and his mother, the Dowager Duchess Charlotte Elizabeth, but his heart was in seeking out people who practiced what Ludwig now called "Christianity of the Heart." Ludwig found many Christians to have fellowship with in Paris, including the head of the Roman Catholic Church there, Cardinal Noailles. At first the cardinal spent many hours trying to convert Ludwig to Catholicism, but eventually he declared that it was wasted effort and instead agreed to focus on the beliefs they held in common and not those that divided them. Ludwig was so delighted to find another man whose heart was ablaze with love for God that he invited the cardinal to join the Order of the Grain of Mustard Seed. The cardinal gratefully accepted the honor, becoming the first Catholic to join the group.

Ludwig's tutor tried hard to convince Ludwig not to spend so much time with religious people. "I am hearing strange rumors about you," he told Ludwig. "No one can understand why you will not accept invitations on Sundays."

"All they need to do is ask me," Ludwig replied. "The answer is plain enough. I will continue to spend Sundays in prayer and Bible study for the benefit of my heart. Let the people think of it what they please."

"And the regent thinks you are a Pietist because you will not gamble or dance with the ladies in his court," Herr Riederer continued.

Ludwig laughed. "And the irony is that the Pietists will not own me because I fellowship with a cardinal! What am I to do?"

"You could try spending more time hunting and conversing with other men of your rank," Herr Riederer answered tersely. "Then I would have better news to report when I return to Gross-Hennersdorf."

"That may be so," Ludwig replied, "but I am no longer in school, and my mother and grandmother did tell me to take up the causes that interested me on my tour. Which reminds me, have you seen the Hotel Dieu Hospital yet?"

"No," Herr Riederer replied.

"You really should come with me this afternoon. It is the most amazing hospital. It accepts even the poorest of the poor. The Christian men who run it are so dedicated. You really must see it. I love to spend time there talking with the patients and the doctors."

Herr Riederer shook his head. "You haven't listened to a word I've said. It will take someone more persuasive than I to shake you from your plans, I can see that."

The two men stayed in Paris for a full year. Ludwig used the opportunity to study English and French and take horse-riding lessons. But by the time September 1720 rolled around, it was well past time for Ludwig to be heading home. Since Ludwig's formal studies were all completed, Herr Riederer left Ludwig in Paris and returned directly home to Saxony. Ludwig was officially done with tutors. Finally he was on his own, and he decided to travel through Switzerland on the way back to his grandmother's castle. He intended to stop along the way at various cities and towns and meet with church leaders. He also wanted to visit his father's two sisters. Both had married into noble families. One was the countess of Polheim, and the other, the countess of Castelle.

Ludwig had met his aunts briefly before, but he was excited to think he would be able to get to know them and their families better. He went first to the countess of Castelle's castle. Her husband had recently died, and Ludwig wanted to see if she needed help of any kind. He soon found that she had little idea about how to handle money or how the estate was run. He set to work untangling the account books and setting up a system she could understand.

The countess of Castelle had two daughters. One of them was eighteen-year-old Theodora, whose help Ludwig enlisted. He told himself that Theodora needed to know how to help her mother after he left. But he had another reason for wanting her to help him, one that Ludwig could scarcely admit to himself. He was falling in love with Theodora. Or at least he thought he was. It was hard to tell, since he had spent so little time around girls his own age.

As the weeks went by, Ludwig became convinced that this pretty, dark-eyed woman would make a wonderful bride. Eventually he got up the courage to talk to his aunt about it. She was delighted with the idea and promised to discuss it with Theodora.

Theodora was shy about the whole matter, but this did not concern Ludwig, who knew that girls of noble birth should not appear too eager to marry. In a flush of enthusiasm Ludwig announced that he was going home to discuss the matter with his mother and grandmother and that if they approved, he would come back in January to become officially betrothed.

Now Ludwig had a real reason to hurry home! When he got back to the castle in late November, he found that several things had changed while he was away. His grandmother had become quite frail, and her sister had moved into the castle to help look after her. His Aunt Henriette had taken over administering the estates of Gross-Hennersdorf and Berthelsdorf. Henriette had even started a small orphanage and home for the poor in Hennersdorf.

Everyone was glad to see Ludwig again. His grandmother was a bit startled to hear of his plans to marry Theodora, but she gave her permission, as did his mother when she visited at Christmastime.

As soon as it was possible, Ludwig set off in a coach for the Black Forest to formally propose to Theodora. Everything went well until they reached the Elster River, which the coach had to cross at a ford near Ebersdorf. The coach was halfway across the ice-cold water when suddenly there was a jolt followed by the cracking sound of breaking wood. The coach then lurched to the left, catapulting the driver into the cold water and leaving Ludwig sprawled on the coach floor. The icy water began to seep in under the door, and Ludwig quickly clambered out and waded ashore. As he looked back, it was obvious what had happened. The coach had hit a large boulder in the river, and the left front wheel had collapsed. Now the coach was stuck in the middle of the ford.

As the coachmen puzzled over what to do, Ludwig recalled that they had passed a castle not far back. He unhitched one of the horses and galloped off to get help. Much to his surprise, he found that the castle belonged to the Reuss family. Ludwig had met one of the sons, Count Henry Reuss, during his stay in Paris. The count had been on a similar grand tour, and the two young men had discovered that they had a lot in common.

As soon as Henry heard of Ludwig's misfortune, he dispatched several servants to drag the coach from the water and pull it back to the castle for repairs.

That night at dinner, Ludwig sat with Henry and Henry's mother and his sister Erdmuth. As they dined, they had a conversation that would alter the course of both Ludwig's and Henry's lives. Henry brought up the subject first.

"Now that I have returned from my trip, my mother thinks it is time for me to marry!" he said, half laughing.

"Have you asked anyone?" Ludwig replied.

Henry shook his head. "There are several young women who are eligible. Let me see, my mother has made many suggestions, but by far my favorite choice would be Countess Theodora von Castelle."

"Oh," interjected Henry's mother, "I think we had better take her off the list. She is no longer available." She smiled a knowing smile at Ludwig.

Ludwig felt his ears turning red. As far as he was aware, no one outside the family knew of the upcoming betrothal, and he had had no idea that his friend Henry also wanted to marry Theodora.

The conversation went on to other things, but Ludwig's mind kept going back to Henry's statement. He tried to recall exactly what Theodora had said to him when he left. Was she as excited about getting married as he was, or had he overlooked her reluctance because of his enthusiasm? What if she was really in love with Henry and did not know how to tell him? Such thoughts troubled him, and by morning Ludwig had made up his mind what to do.

"Henry," he said, as the two young men met walking down the stone staircase to breakfast, "I have something I must tell you. I am on my way to the Castelle castle to become officially betrothed to the Countess Theodora.

"But," spluttered Henry, "how do you know her?"

"She is my cousin," Ludwig replied, "but that is not the point."

"Then what is?" Henry asked, looking thoroughly confused and embarrassed.

"I cannot get betrothed to her knowing how highly you think of her and not knowing how she thinks of you. If she thinks as highly of you as you think of her, I will gladly step aside and allow love to take its true course."

"What are you saying?" Henry asked as he stopped at the bottom of the stairs.

"What I am saying," Ludwig said carefully, "is that you must accompany me to Castelle castle and we will ask Theodora which of us she would prefer to marry."

"No, I would not think of it. Not if you have an arrangement already," Henry exclaimed.

"And I wouldn't think of continuing with our plans until I knew for sure that that is what she wants. So the matter is settled. As soon as the coach is fixed, we will be on our way."

And so they were. The two young men arrived at Castelle castle and were met by a very surprised Theodora. Ludwig explained to her what had happened, and she tearfully confessed she had secretly been in love with Henry for some time but had been too nervous to bring up the matter with Ludwig.

"It is settled then," Ludwig said. "God's will be done. I wish you two every happiness."

On March 9 a formal church service was held to announce the betrothal of the Countess Theodora to Count Henry Reuss. Ludwig overcame his heartache and even wrote a cantata, which he performed at the service. He left soon after the service ended, having seen his cousin happily betrothed, but not to him.

All of this gave Ludwig serious pause for thought. He decided not to look for a wife again but to pray and wait for God to bring the right woman to him. In the meantime he had plenty of other things to keep him busy.

Ever since he could recall, Ludwig had wanted to become a Lutheran minister, and his tour of Europe had made him even more certain that this was his destiny. There was just one problem. Both his mother and his grandmother were completely opposed to the idea. It simply was not appropriate for a count, especially one of the highest order as Ludwig was, to lower himself to become a pastor. There was no room for discussion of the matter with either woman. A count could become a patron of church work but never a church worker. To pursue his calling, Ludwig would have to disobey them, and this was something he could not in all conscience do. He reminded himself that the fifth commandment was "Honor thy father and mother" and that that was what he must do.

Instead, Ludwig followed his grandmother's wishes and became a counselor in the court of Augustus the Strong, King of Saxony. This was an important position and required Ludwig to move to Dresden. However, even while a counselor in the royal court, Ludwig spent all of his spare time and all day Sunday reading and praying and writing.

In May 1721 Ludwig came of age and received the inheritance his father had left him. It was a considerable amount of money, and after praying and thinking hard, Ludwig decided to buy the estate of Berthelsdorf from his grandmother.

The estate consisted of a rambling, rundown village, a Lutheran church, and several farms. Ludwig hoped that one day he might be able to turn it into a small Christian community. As he looked out over the forested hills and valleys of his new estate, he had no idea that he was standing on a piece of ground that would one day make him famous—as well as an outlaw.

Chapter 5

# Herrnhut

Ludwig made Johann Heitz, a pietistic Swiss man, the manager of his new estate, and in April 1722 he appointed John Rothe to become the Lutheran pastor of the Berthelsdorf parish. At the time of the appointment, he told John, "I bought this estate because I wanted to spend my life among peasants and win their souls for Christ. So go, Rothe, to the vineyard of the Lord. You will find in me a brother and helper rather than a patron."

Not long after John was appointed, he visited Ludwig, bringing with him a friend he introduced as Christian David. Christian was ten years older than Ludwig and had been born in Moravia, a region located about two hundred miles southeast of Saxony. At age twenty-seven he had become a Christian while staying in Görlitz, Saxony.

After his conversion, Christian had begun making preaching tours back to Moravia, where he came upon a number of persecuted Christians who were descended from a group known as the Unitas Fratrum, or the Unity of the Brethren. Ludwig had not heard of this tiny group before and was eager to learn all about it. Christian told him that the Unitas Fratrum traced its roots back to the teachings of the reformer Jan Hus, who was burned at the stake as a heretic in Prague in 1415. Although the group had been persecuted throughout most of its existence, after the Reformation its persecution by the Catholic Church had become even more intense.

"Count Zinzendorf," Christian began respectfully, "a group of these Christians calling themselves the Hidden Seed seek a place where they might settle and practice their beliefs unhindered by the religious authorities. I am told that you might let some of these people come and settle on your Berthelsdorf estate."

Ludwig thought back to the vow he had taken in the Order of the Grain of Mustard Seed. He had pledged to do good to his fellow men. And here he was hearing about a downtrodden and persecuted group of Christians. What else could he say but yes?

"I will give them land to build on, and Christ will give them rest," Ludwig told Christian.

Ludwig did not think too much more about his conversation with Christian. His work in Dresden occupied much of his time. The chancellor kept him busy negotiating settlements between citizens and sorting out land claims. But although there was a lot of work to do, the work was relatively easy, and as the months rolled by, Ludwig became bored with it. He constantly reminded himself that he was honoring his mother and grandmother's wishes and that one day God would give him the desires of his heart. To help him through this time, he turned to writing hymns to express how he felt. He was especially pleased with one hymn he wrote called "Jesus, Still Lead On." The hymn's verses read,

> Jesus, lead us on till our rest is won;
> And although the way be cheerless,
> We will follow, calm and fearless.
> Guide us by Your hand
> To our fatherland.
>
> If the way be drear,
> If the foe be near,
> Let not faithless fears o'ertake us;
> Let not faith and hope forsake us,
> For through many a woe
> To our home we go.

For Ludwig, life in Dresden was for the most part cheerless and dreary, except for one thing that kept him going—his Sunday-afternoon meetings. The meetings, which were held in his apartment, started at three in the afternoon and lasted for four hours. Anyone, whether a peasant or a nobleman, was welcome to attend, both those who were searching for truth and those who were firm believers in Christ. Ludwig would lead the people as they read the New Testament together, prayed, and discussed religious topics. And although Ludwig had always loved to talk about spiritual issues, this was the first time he really had had the opportunity to listen to people from lower social classes. Even though these people did not know Greek, Hebrew, or Latin, Ludwig was impressed with many of their insights into the Bible. The thought that everyone, rich or poor, educated or illiterate, noble or commoner, had something to contribute to the meeting surprised and then delighted Ludwig and inspired him to keep going through the dreary weeks.

Although he would have liked to visit Berthelsdorf more often, Ludwig was happy with the way things were progressing there. He was confident that in Johann Heitz and John Rothe he had found the right men for the job of overseeing the managerial and spiritual needs of his estate. Both men were also good letter writers, and they kept Ludwig up to date with what was happening at his new estate.

In early June, Ludwig received a letter from Johann reporting that Christian had returned from Moravia with the Neisser family. Ludwig was surprised at how fast Christian had moved. He had expected it would be many months before any Christians from Moravia arrived at his estate.

Johann also reported that he had set aside a patch of land about a mile from the village for the new arrivals to live on. He had chosen this spot because it was on the highway between Lobau and

Zittau. Since the Neisser brothers were cutlers by trade, making and repairing knives and farm instruments, Johann thought that they would be better off carrying on their business near a steady stream of passersby.

The place where the new refugees from Moravia were located was known as Hutberg, or Watch Hill, and in his enthusiasm, Johann told Ludwig that he had named the place Herrnhut. Explaining the choice, he wrote:

> May God grant that your excellency may be able to build on the hill called the Hutberg a town which may not only itself abide under the Lord's Watch [*Herrn-hut*], but all the inhabitants of which may also continue on the Lord's Watch, so that no silence may be there by day or night.

As the days went by, Ludwig found himself thinking more and more about the refugees at Herrnhut. How were they faring in the unusually wet summer? Had they made friends with the local people at Berthelsdorf? And most of all, what would their future hold?

Ludwig also thought about his own future. He had adjusted to the idea of not marrying Theodora, but he still wanted to get married. This time, however, he prayed hard before he asked someone.

The woman he had in mind was Countess Erdmuth Reuss, the sister of Count Henry Reuss, who had married Theodora. Ludwig had spoken to her a little when he had first visited Ebersdorf. He had been back several times since then to visit Henry and Theodora. On these visits he found himself looking forward to seeing Erdmuth. She was a tall, attractive woman with high, arched eyebrows and an oval face. She was intelligent, like his mother and grandmother, but what Ludwig liked most was the way she lived out her faith. For once he had found someone with a reputation for being more pious than he was! Erdmuth and her older sister Benigna were well known both for the wonderful Christian services they held at the castle for their workers and for their kindness to friends and strangers alike.

All of these traits impressed Ludwig greatly, and he felt sure he had found the right bride this time. He wrote to Erdmuth's mother expressing his desire to marry her daughter. Trying to be as honest as he could about his uncertain future and his passion to live for God, he wrote,

> I foresee many difficulties in this case: I am but a poor acquisition for any person, and the dear Countess Erdmuth must not only enter upon a life of self-denial with me, but also co-operate with me in my principal design, namely, to assist men in gaining souls for Christ, under shame and reproach, if she will be of any service to me.

Erdmuth herself wrote back to say that she was more than willing to follow Ludwig in whatever he felt led to do. This was a huge relief to Ludwig, and a wedding date was set for September 7, 1722. The couple were married by the court chaplain at the Reuss castle in Ebersdorf. Ludwig was twenty-two years old and Erdmuth twenty-one.

The newlyweds stayed at Ebersdorf for several weeks after the wedding before returning to Dresden, where Ludwig again took up the task of court adviser. Ludwig and Erdmuth rented an apartment from the local burgomaster and set up home. As part of her wedding gift, Baroness von Gersdorf sent the couple lavish furniture. She also sent a letter to Erdmuth, welcoming her to the family and expressing her hope that they would meet soon.

It wasn't until December 2, 1722, that Ludwig was free enough from his court responsibilities to make the trip back to Berthelsdorf with his new wife. He wanted to spend the Christmas season with his family and also look over plans for a mansion that he planned to build there for him and Erdmuth. His old friend and fellow member of the Order of the Grain of Mustard Seed, Frederick von Watteville, happened to be visiting Dresden, and he went along with them.

Tall pine and beech trees cast shadows over the road as the three weary travelers made their way toward Berthelsdorf. By the time they neared their destination, the sun had set and darkness enveloped them. As they rode along, Ludwig noticed a light shining through the thick trees.

"Stop," Ludwig called to the coach driver. "I wish to investigate something." He then turned to Erdmuth and Frederick. "See that light in the woods?

If I am not mistaken, that is the new home where the Neisser family from Moravia has settled. Let us find the path to their house."

Ludwig climbed from the coach and walked ahead a little farther. The full moon rising above the trees gave him ample light to see.

"Here it is," Ludwig said, motioning to the other two. Then he turned to the driver. "You stay here. We won't be long."

Erdmuth and Frederick followed Ludwig as he led them into the frozen woods until they came to a two-story wooden cottage. Ludwig knocked at the door. Immediately he heard the sound of little feet running, and a small boy about seven years old opened the door. The boy's eyes grew wide as he looked at Ludwig's elaborate clothes.

"Hello, young man," Ludwig said, patting the boy's head.

A woman came up behind the boy and curtsied deeply when she saw the three travelers.

Soon they were all seated beside the fire. Augustine and Martha Neisser introduced themselves, as did Augustine's brother, Jacob, Jacob's wife, Anna, and their son Wenzel.

"I thought you had more children," Ludwig said. "Twins perhaps?"

Jacob reached for his wife's hand. "We did, sir," he replied. "But the Lord saw fit to take the twin babies home last month, and then a week ago our three-year-old daughter, Anna, suffered greatly from water on the lungs and did not recover."

"I am sorry to hear that," Erdmuth said. "It is very difficult to accept these things, but the Lord's will be done."

"Yes," Jacob agreed. "Even though we have endured great trials, we are sure that God has led us here. I don't step outside this cottage without thinking of the words of my grandfather, George Jaeschke. As he saw the angel of death draw near to him fifteen years ago, he gathered his family together and said this to us: 'It is true that our liberties are gone and that our descendants are giving way to a worldly spirit.... It may seem as though the final end of the Brethren's Church has come. But, my beloved children, you will see a great deliverance. The remnant will be saved. How, I cannot say, but something tells me that an exodus will take place and that a refuge will be offered in a country and on a spot where you will be able, without fear, to serve the Lord according to His holy Word. Take care that when the exodus begins, you are among the first to leave. Do not wait until last. Remember what I have told you.'"

Ludwig was greatly moved when he heard these words. "You are very welcome to live here and to practice your religion free from harm," he said. "Now I would like to pray for you all."

With that he knelt on the wood floor. Everyone else in the room quickly joined him, and Ludwig prayed that God would protect and guide this family, who had already endured so much.

The following day, Christian and Johann took Ludwig and Frederick out to show them the plans they had for the development of Herrnhut. Christian was so excited that he could hardly get the words out in the right order. He talked of a large city rising out of the hills, with wide streets, paved courtyards, and a library, school, hospital, and printing house.

Ludwig privately thought that the plan was mostly Christian's wild imagination. He wasn't convinced that any other refugees would join the Neissers. However, Ludwig did not account for Christian's passion to lead Protestants out of the persecution they were facing at the hands of Catholic priests and nobility.

Christian returned to Moravia to urge other members of the Neisser family to join their brothers at Herrnhut. Eighteen more pilgrims set out in the dead of night with nothing but the clothes on their backs and a few loaves of bread. Word of what Christian was doing traveled fast, and he soon learned that in retaliation angry Catholics had burned his house to the ground. But this did not stop him; on the contrary, he went from town to town urging others to flee with him.

Ludwig and Erdmuth had to return to Dresden, but letters from Johann kept Ludwig up to date about the new arrivals at Herrnhut and many of their stunning stories of escape. Some of the people had been imprisoned and later found their chains broken or their locked doors mysteriously open. One man who had been imprisoned in a castle had found some rope hidden in his cell and used it to climb down three stories to the ground. All of this thrilled Ludwig. The sacrifices the people had made and their miraculous escape stories reminded him of events in the book of Acts.

Johann also sent regular reports on more mundane issues, including progress on the mansion, which was slowly taking shape. Many of the new refugees were employed on the project as carpenters and masons.

Finally, in August 1723, after many delays, the Zinzendorf mansion was ready to move into. Ludwig took leave of the royal court for the summer, and he and Erdmuth hurried to Berthelsdorf to see their new home, a huge, square, four-story house, which Ludwig named Bethel. On the door lintel Ludwig had inscribed in gold lettering the words

> Here we spend the night as guests:
> Therefore this house is neither beautiful nor permanent.
> Quite right: we have also another house
> In heaven where things are different.

Along with these words were inscribed the Bible references of Zechariah 9:12 and 2 Corinthians 5:1–2.

Ludwig had lost none of his religious zeal while he was in Dresden. In fact, the opposite had occurred. The more Ludwig saw of court life there, the more he longed to be involved in Christian work. And now that he was back in Berthelsdorf for some months, he set to work putting several of his plans into action.

To do this, Ludwig realized that he needed a small team of committed people to help. Just as he had done while a student at the Paedagogium, he invited others to join him. The three people he asked were Frederick von Watteville, who had been staying with Ludwig since the previous Christmas; John Rothe, the Berthelsdorf pastor; and Melchior Schaeffer, pastor of the neighboring parish. The men called themselves the Covenant of the Four Brethren, and they and their wives pledged to live holy lives, encourage others to do the same, work for religious revival, publish Christian literature, and establish Christian schools.

Having made this commitment to one another, the Four Brethren got to work. They hired a printer named Gottlieb Ludwig and prepared to set up a press at Berthelsdorf. This proved to be a difficult task, however. The Saxon royal court did not appreciate anyone's, not even a member of the court, having the ability to publish reading material, and it forbade Ludwig to set up a printing press anywhere in Saxony.

The four were not easily defeated, however, and they came up with a plan to set up the printing press at Ebersdorf under the watchful eye of Count Henry Reuss. Ebersdorf was in the province of Kostritz, not in Saxony, and the rulers of Kostritz did not object to having a printing press in their realm.

Plans were also developed for a charity school and a school for girls at Berthelsdorf. These were built with a generous gift from Lady Johanna von

Zezschwitz, whom Frederick married soon after construction began.

Ludwig had another plan too. He wanted to build a school like the Paedagogium for the sons of noblemen. The other three men agreed with him, and so on May 12, 1724, everyone at Berthelsdorf arrived at the construction site to watch Ludwig lay the foundation stone for the school and hear him preach a sermon. This was supposed to be an important day, and it turned out to be just that. But the most important event had little to do with laying the foundation stone. It had to do with the five strangers who walked over the hill just as the ceremony was about to begin. These five men were destined to change the Herrnhut community forever.

Chapter 6

# Growing Pains

"Greetings, Count Zinzendorf. I am Melchior Zeisberger."

"I am John Töltschig."

"I am David Nitschmann."

"And I am David Nitschmann."

"And I also am David Nitschmann."

Each man stepped forward and bowed as he introduced himself.

Ludwig searched the men's faces to see if they were playing some kind of joke on him. Could all three men possibly have the same name?

The David Nitschmann who had introduced himself first seemed to sense Ludwig's confusion. "We are all called David Nitschmann," he said. "It may help you to remember that this David is a carpenter, and this David a weaver." He pointed to the two other David Nitschmanns as he spoke.

"Thank you," Ludwig said. "Now, you must tell me why you have come here. Did you follow Christian David?"

"Not exactly," David Nitschmann the weaver replied. "We are fleeing from Zauchenthal, Moravia, and are on our way to Lissa, Poland, where a remnant from the Unitas Fratrum settled decades ago. When Christian passed through our town and told us about Herrnhut, we decided to come and see the place for ourselves on our way."

"We are glad to welcome you," Ludwig replied. "However, I must excuse myself. We are about to begin a dedication service. Please stay and join us."

Soon the service began. The gathered group sang several hymns, and then Ludwig preached his sermon and said a prayer of dedication over the foundation stone. During the prayer he petitioned, "God bless this undertaking if it prove useful to You, but destroy it now at the beginning if it is mere human plan and action."

When the service was over, Ludwig talked some more with the young men from Zauchenthal.

"We were touched by the words of your prayer," Melchior said. "It is clear that God is among you."

"We sincerely hope so, or our work is in vain," Ludwig replied. "Now, tell me more about yourselves."

The five men were all sons of well-to-do parents. They told Ludwig that during the previous months they had been leading an evangelical revival in their town. But eventually things had come to a head, and the five were dragged before a judge, who happened to be John Töltschig's father. The judge ordered the men to close down their religious meetings and follow the example of the other young men in town, who were not bothered with religion but enjoyed dancing and carousing in the local taverns. He also warned them against trying to flee from Moravia for some more religiously tolerant place. He pointed out that the authorities took a dim view of people who tried to emigrate from their realm for religious reasons, and the young men would be dealt with harshly if they were caught fleeing. Yet after facing the judge, the five men could see no alternative but to flee. So the next night they set out on their journey.

When he heard their story, Ludwig urged the five young men to stay on at Herrnhut for a few days. The five accepted the invitation and several days later asked Ludwig if they could all live permanently at Herrnhut. They explained that they had found everything they hoped to find in Poland right there at Herrnhut and wanted to stay and become part of the community. Ludwig gladly agreed to take them in.

Eventually Ludwig and Erdmuth had to leave the growing community at Berthelsdorf and return to Dresden, where Ludwig was required to once again take up his responsibilities in the royal court. One happy event that broke the boredom Ludwig felt upon returning to Dresden was the arrival of Christian Ernst von Zinzendorf, to whom Erdmuth gave birth on August 7, 1724. Ludwig wrote to Johann Heitz to tell him the good news. The reply he received back was devastating.

The community at Herrnhut, which now numbered ninety, was in shambles. At first the refugees had all worked to help one another and shared what they had. But now, Johann reported, it was every man for himself. So many different languages were spoken and so many brands of religion from Calvinist to Catholic were practiced at Herrnhut that no one could agree on anything. It had been a tradition that when new refugees arrived, someone would blow a horn and the community would gather in the square to greet them and offer help. But not anymore. Ludwig read how no one now came at the sound of the horn. In fact, new refugees were often heckled and told they were not welcome, that there was not enough housing or jobs for them and they had better move on. Ludwig's dream of a loving Christian community was fast devolving into a nightmare.

By November 1724 Ludwig knew that he had a crisis on his hands. It could not have come at a worse time. Baby Christian Ernst was sickly, and the doctor declared that he would not survive the winter. In fact, he did not survive another week. The Zinzendorfs buried their firstborn son, and then Ludwig hurried off to Berthelsdorf to see what could be done about the situation at Herrnhut.

As soon as he arrived at his estate, Ludwig began interviewing the refugees to see what their complaints were against one another and how he could help solve them. He interviewed residents for three days and nights in a row, pausing only between the hours of two and five in the morning for a quick nap. More than anything, he wanted to work out a way to turn the situation around.

Once the interviews were over, Ludwig and the other members of the Four Brethren came up with a plan based on the idea of "helpers." Helpers were members of the Herrnhut community or the Berthelsdorf church who had proven that they were loyal, kind, and committed to God. Age, social rank, and wealth were not important. Ludwig believed that all men and women were equal in the sight of God.

Each helper was given a specific task. A tailor and a gardener were made religious teachers. Augustine Neisser was appointed as an almoner, and Jacob and Anna Neisser were appointed as encouragers. Christian David, a sixteen-year-old cowherd named Anna-Lena, and a lame teenage boy were made helpers of the sick. Every job was clearly laid out. The almoner was in charge of all the poor people, those who begged for alms. His job was to help them find employment and a place to live. The helpers of the sick were responsible for visiting all of the sick people in the community each day, bringing them medicine and bathing them.

Some members of Herrnhut objected to being told what to do by those they considered beneath them. They questioned what right a sixteen-year-old girl had to tell them what to do and challenged the idea of making someone as common as a tailor a religious teacher. But Ludwig held firm. While the world outside recognized people's wealth, social position, and sex, he insisted that these rankings had no place in a community of Christians.

All of this organization took a lot of work on Ludwig's part, especially when some members of the Herrnhut community argued against and objected to everything he did. Even some of the people closest to Ludwig questioned his effort in trying to start such a different type of community. Couldn't he see that Herrnhut was eventually doomed to fail, no matter how hard he tried to keep it together? So why not just evict all the troublemakers and malcontents and keep only those who were quiet, obedient workers?

Whenever such questions came up, Ludwig always gave the same answer. "I could use my power as a landlord to make them all leave," he would say, "but I have a firm belief that God has gathered these people here for a reason, and I will wait patiently to see what good He brings through them."

The work continued, with Ludwig spending as much time at Herrnhut as he could while still fulfilling his duties in the royal court.

As life at the Herrnhut community began to settle into a new pattern, several industries sprang up based upon the various skills of new arrivals. Martin and Leonard Dober, two brothers from Swabia, were expert potters, and they set up wheels and a kiln and were soon selling their pottery. A linen weaver arrived too, and his looms provided work for many of the refugees.

Although it seemed that Herrnhut might be saved after all, opposition from the outside was steadily growing against it. In July 1726, Ludwig, Erdmuth, and their new baby daughter, Benigna, were staying in Berthelsdorf following the death of Ludwig's grandmother, Countess von Gersdorf. While they were there, word came that David Nitschmann had been taken prisoner. David had secretly traveled to Kremsir, Moravia, to bring his father back to Herrnhut. While there he had been captured and was being held without trial under suspicion of inciting refugees to emigrate.

Ludwig knew that he had to do something about the situation. The entire question of emigration was becoming tenser by the day. In August 1726 Ludwig traveled to Kremsir to meet with the Catholic cardinal there and the cardinal's brother, an officer in the Austrian Imperial Service. Ludwig hoped that they would accept his argument that a 1648 pact called the Treaty of Westphalia established equality of rights for both Protestants and Catholics, and therefore Christians who so desired had the right to emigrate.

The meeting did not go smoothly for Ludwig. Although the cardinal and his brother were polite, they were also firm. They had no intention of releasing David from prison, nor would they allow Ludwig to visit him. Ludwig tried everything he knew to make the two men change their minds, but it was no use. Eventually he returned to Herrnhut discouraged and worried about David's fate. Little did he imagine the problems he would encounter after he arrived home.

A man named Johann Krüger, who had been a court preacher, came to live in the village. He announced that everyone should separate himself from Pastor Rothe and the Lutheran Church. This caused a split in the community, and soon those who followed Krüger shunned those who did not accept what he said. As more people began listening to what Krüger had to say, he became more outrageous. He accused Ludwig of being the "Beast" and John Rothe of being a "False Prophet." And as unbelievable as it seemed to Ludwig, Krüger even managed to persuade Christian David over to his way of thinking.

This new state of affairs appalled Ludwig, but he still refused to evict the refugees from his land. Instead he wrote hymns and prayed that God would intervene and do something to reunite the divided community.

Something did happen. By January 1727 Johann Krüger had gone insane. He began ranting and raving, pulling his hair out, and cutting himself. Suddenly his followers could see for themselves that he was mentally unbalanced, and Krüger soon left Herrnhut for good.

Johann Krüger's leaving did not automatically heal the deep rifts that had developed. In fact, the whole community was in the worst shape it had ever been in. Hatred and gossip abounded, and Ludwig felt that he had to do something drastic if he was to pull it back on track. He quit his job in the royal court in Dresden and moved his family into the mansion at Berthelsdorf to live permanently. He announced that John Rothe would continue in his role as pastor of the Berthelsdorf parish while Ludwig would take over the role of assistant pastor to those at the Herrnhut community. He knew that many people would raise their eyebrows at this, but Ludwig did not care. All that mattered to him was not letting the opportunity to create a godly community slip away.

Once Ludwig moved to Berthelsdorf, his days were full. He went to Herrnhut each day to pray with people, listen to their grievances, and hold Bible studies. As he did this, he felt the tide slowly begin to turn.

On May 11, 1727, the community held a *Singstunde,* or singing meeting. The following afternoon Ludwig again gathered the community together. He spoke to the gathered crowd for three hours about how wrong it was to allow small things to divide them and how, if they all served Christ Jesus, they should be able to get along.

Ludwig introduced two documents he had been writing. The first was the *Manorial Injunctions and Prohibitions,* in which he, as owner of the estate, laid out the laws that everyone living at Herrnhut was obliged to abide by. The second document was called *The Brotherly Agreement of the Brethren from Bohemia and Moravia and Others, Binding Them to Walk According to the Apostolic Rule.* This document had been written in collaboration with a number of the members of the Herrnhut community. It was a voluntary agreement that bound the members together in Christian fellowship. It contained forty-two principles, which Ludwig read aloud one by one.

When he had finished reading, Ludwig invited those gathered to come up one at a time and shake his hand if they agreed to abide by the principles. Slowly, members of the community stood and walked to the front. Many of them broke down and wept as they shook Ludwig's hand. They apologized to him and to one another for their behavior. Christian David, who had been swept away by Johann Krüger's teaching, wept openly on Ludwig's shoulder as he asked him for forgiveness.

When the meeting finally returned to some sort of order, the people wanted to elect elders to help them stick to their new commitment. Twelve elders were chosen, among them the two Neisser brothers, a seventy-year-old joiner, a twenty-five-year-old cobbler, and a carpenter. Ludwig read the passage from the book of Acts about how Jesus' eleven disciples drew lots to choose another man to join their number and replace Judas. He put the names of the twelve elders they had just chosen into a basket, which he prayed over. He then pulled out four names: Christian David, George Nitschmann, Christopher Hoffman, and Melchior Zeisberger. These men were to be the chief elders.

Ludwig was delighted that Christian David had been chosen, even though Christian had been disloyal and persuaded by Johann Krüger to accuse Ludwig of the worst possible things. He explained to Erdmuth why he felt that way.

"Although our dear Christian David was calling me the Beast and Mr. Rothe the False Prophet, we could see his honest heart nevertheless and knew we could lead him right. It is not a bad maxim when honest men are going wrong to put them into office, and they will learn from experience what they will never learn from speculation."

Ludwig was chosen by the group to be warden. He decided that it was time to sacrifice the comfort of his mansion and suggested that his family move directly into the Herrnhut community. The members of the community gladly accepted his suggestion, and Ludwig began preparations to have a modest home built right away.

Things in the community changed that day. People became more accepting of one another. They listened to one another, and instead of getting into arguments, they agreed to respect each other's opinions.

Finally, on Saturday, July 1, Ludwig, Erdmuth, and one-year-old Benigna moved into the new house at Herrnhut. It was a particularly trying move for Erdmuth. The weather was very hot, and she was expecting another baby in two months. And the house was not even fully built. The plaster on the walls was still wet. But Ludwig wanted to be moved into the house before Sunday, since Sundays had become a day of celebration at Herrnhut and Berthelsdorf. People from all over the province flocked to hear Pastor Rothe's teaching and to see for themselves the wonderful things that were happening at the community.

Chapter 7

# Hidden Seed

Much to Ludwig's delight, the situation at Herrnhut continued to improve. Small groups called bands were established. These groups consisted of two to eight people who met together regularly for Bible study, prayer, and singing. The bands had a marked effect on the community. Everywhere Ludwig went he saw community members huddled together encouraging one another and praying about problems as they arose. How different this atmosphere was from a year ago, when everyone was consumed with the doctrines that divided them.

On July 22, 1727, Ludwig had decided that the community was doing so well that he could take time off to visit his great uncle, Baron Gersdorf, in

Hartmannsdorf, Silesia. On the way he stopped in the town of Zittau and paid a visit to the local reference library. Despite having read most theology books of the day, Ludwig discovered in the library an old, dusty book with the title *Ratio Disciplinae (Account of Discipline)* engraved on its leather spine. He pulled the book from the shelf, cracked it open, and began to read. He could scarcely put it down. The book was a Latin version of the constitution of the Unitas Fratrum, and to Ludwig's surprise, the principles laid out within its pages bore a remarkable likeness to the principles the Herrnhut community had recently embraced.

At the front of the book was a history of the Unity of the Brethren written by Bishop John Amos Comenius. What Ludwig read here stunned him. Ludwig had thought of the refugees from Moravia as people seeking a place where they could practice their Christian beliefs free from persecution. The people had talked of being the hidden seed of an ancient group, but he had shepherded them into the Lutheran Church and encouraged them to think of themselves as a church within a church. But now he was reading that they actually belonged to a fully formed Protestant church that was older than the Lutheran Church! The Unitas Fratrum had been founded in 1457—sixty years before Martin Luther nailed his ninety-five theses to the church door in Wittenberg. In fact, by the time of Luther, the Unitas Fratrum had some four hundred congregations and nearly two hundred thousand followers.

Ludwig translated an excerpt from *Ratio Disciplinae* from Latin to German to take back to Herrnhut to show to the refugees from Moravia.

While he visited his uncle, Ludwig thought long and hard on all he had read about the Unitas Fratrum. Did God have a bigger plan for this group? Were these people living on his estate for more than just protection from persecution? Ludwig could not get these questions out of his mind. It was true that they called themselves the Hidden Seed, but what was that seed supposed to grow into? Perhaps they had been guided to Berthelsdorf for a greater purpose. Perhaps God wanted to revive and breathe new life into this oldest of Protestant denominations. And perhaps Herrnhut was the beginning of that revival.

Before Ludwig left his uncle's estate, he offered a prayer of dedication. "I, as far as I can, will help to bring about this renewal. And though I have to sacrifice my earthly possessions, my honors, my life, as long as I live I will do my utmost to see to it that the little company of the Lord's disciples shall be preserved for Him until He comes," he prayed.

Ludwig arrived back at Herrnhut on August 4. When he showed the Moravians the excerpt he had taken from the *Ratio Disciplinae,* they became very excited. They, too, recognized the similarities between the precepts of the *Ratio Disciplinae* and the guiding principles they had recently subscribed to in *The Brotherly Agreement of the Brethren from Bohemia and Moravia and Others, Binding Them to Walk According to the Apostolic Rule.*

This was the first time that most of the refugees from Moravia had heard any of the details of the church their forefathers had founded. Through years of persecution they had been cut off from other members of the Unitas Fratrum and from books that explained the group's history and beliefs. Now they understood their past, and they were ready to look to their future. They were the Hidden Seed. To guide their community, they had put in place principles that were almost identical to the principles that guided their forefathers. Surely, they marveled, only God could have guided them to do this. They thanked Him and rejoiced and eagerly anticipated the revival of the Unitas Fratrum.

On Sunday August 10, Pastor Rothe came to Herrnhut to conduct the afternoon service. Partway through the sermon, Ludwig watched as the pastor sank to his knees and began to pray fervently. Those gathered for the service followed his lead and knelt and began to pray. They stayed on their knees, praying until after midnight.

The following morning John Rothe returned to invite the Herrnhut community to a communion service at the Berthelsdorf church on Wednesday. Because Ludwig felt that this would be an important meeting, he went from house to house throughout the community encouraging all to attend.

On Wednesday morning Pastor Rothe came to Herrnhut and delivered a sermon on the significance and importance of communion. Following his sermon, the members of the community walked the mile to the Berthelsdorf church. By the time the communion service began, the church was packed. A hymn was sung to open the meeting, and then John prayed a blessing over two girls who were being confirmed.

Following the confirmation the congregation knelt and began to sing, "My soul before Thee prostrate lies, To Thee, its source, my spirit flies." As the people sang, Ludwig noticed that some of them were beginning to weep. A powerful wave of emotion seemed to sweep over the place, and soon the sound of people crying drowned out the singing.

When the hymn was over, Ludwig led in a prayer. He prayed for true unity among those gathered for the service and that those in the Herrnhut community would have no more disagreements but rather would find new vigor and oneness in their relationship with Jesus Christ. When he was finished, several others prayed. Before long the weeping had given way to fervent prayer as people poured out their hearts to God.

When the service finally came to an end, no one wanted to leave. Outside the church, people gathered and talked about what they had just experienced and how they felt a new closeness to God and to each other. Slowly they drifted into groups and continued to talk and pray and sing hymns.

As the afternoon wore on, Ludwig sent for food to feed the group. When it arrived, the food was distributed, and the people ate together. The scene reminded Ludwig of something from the early church in the New Testament, where the members would gather regularly for love feasts. He wondered whether perhaps, like those early Christians, the members of the Herrnhut community could make the love feast a regular part of their worship together.

Two weeks later, on August 27, to keep alive the new closeness they felt to God, twenty-eight men and twenty-eight women from Herrnhut pledged themselves to each spend one hour a day in prayer. They drew lots as to which hour they should pray, so that at any time of the day or night, two people were praying for Herrnhut and for the world.

Singing also became a vital part of everyday life. Ludwig believed that hymns could be sung as prayers once they were known by heart. He encouraged everyone at Herrnhut to memorize hundreds of hymns. Soon the only people who needed hymnals were visitors to the community. The members of the community sang for hours at a time. The person leading a service would often create entire sermons by selecting various verses around a theme from hundreds of hymns. He would begin singing, and as soon as the congregation recognized the verse of a particular hymn, they would join in.

Ludwig also introduced the "Daily Watchword," a Bible verse selected by lot the night before. Everyone in the community was encouraged to recite it to one another and think about its meaning throughout the day.

News of what was happening at Herrnhut soon spread far and wide. Ludwig began receiving up to fifty letters a day asking if men and women from the community could come to their churches and talk about their experiences. Members of Herrnhut responded enthusiastically to these requests.

Soon people from the community were traveling as far away as Italy and England to speak. In most places they visited, they were forbidden from preaching directly to the congregation. Instead they gathered together small groups of like-minded Christians and told them about Herrnhut and all God was doing among them. They then encouraged the people to put aside their differences and act as one united church.

On September 19, 1727, in the midst of this new direction and activity, Erdmuth gave birth to a son. Ludwig named him Christian Renatus in honor of their first child who had died nearly three years before.

The community continued to prosper. More houses and buildings were erected, and the choir system was developed. Under this system, every person living at Herrnhut was assigned to a group, or choir, according to his or her age, sex, and marital status. The first choir established was the single men's choir. This was a particularly active group, and the men decided to live together in their own large house and help one another with their work. This choir became a center for handcraft industries. In their spare time in the evenings, the young men devoted themselves to studying other languages, medicine, and geography.

The single sisters' choir was led by teenaged Anna Nitschmann. Although she was one of the youngest single girls, she demonstrated a particularly mature Christian attitude. The single girls also lived together in their own large house.

Other choirs were established for married couples, widows, widowers, girls, boys, and even infants. And since all those in the choir had pledged themselves to help the others in the group, it was not difficult for men and women to be away traveling. While they were away, the other members of their choir would cover for them at Herrnhut, helping to do their share of the physical work or watching over their children for them.

In 1729 Ludwig received the news that thirty-one-year-old David Nitschmann had died in prison, where he had languished for three years after Ludwig's attempt to win his freedom. The news saddened Ludwig. David had shown such promise as a leader in the Herrnhut community.

Erdmuth gave birth to a fourth child on September 18, 1729. It was another son, whom they named Christian Friedrich. Sadly, the baby was sickly from the beginning, and he died when he was four weeks old. About a year later, in October 1730, Erdmuth gave birth to yet another son, whom they named Theodore and who appeared to be a strong and healthy baby.

The following April, Ludwig, accompanied by David Nitschmann the carpenter and two other Moravian men, set out for Denmark for the coronation of King Christian VI. In Copenhagen, Ludwig experienced the usual round of pomp and ceremony for a person of his social position. Much to Ludwig's surprise, the new king awarded Ludwig the Cross of the Order of the Knights of Danebrog in honor of his contribution to religion. Ludwig also dined with heads of state who had been invited from all over Europe to the coronation.

It was not a rich or powerful person, however, who made the biggest impression on Ludwig while he was in Copenhagen. The person who captivated Ludwig's attention was the servant of his friend Count Laurwig. This servant's simple story set in motion a series of events that would see people from the Herrnhut community spread around the world.

Chapter 8

# Sending Out Missionaries

"Where did you get your servant?" Ludwig asked Count Laurwig during dinner.

"His name is Anthony Ulrich, and I brought him here from Saint Thomas in the Caribbean," the count replied. "I was there a year ago, and he struck me as a good worker. He is intelligent, speaks fluent Dutch, and has more than proved his worth to me. He has even become a sincere Christian."

Ludwig's ears perked up at this last comment. He wanted to know how this muscular man with jet-black skin and an open, assured look on his face had become a Christian. Ludwig's opportunity to find out came as Anthony was removing his empty dinner plate.

"Count Laurwig tells me you have become a Christian since coming with him to Europe. Tell me, how did you come to hear of Christ?" Ludwig asked.

Anthony looked surprised that one of the dinner guests would ask him questions of a personal nature, but then his eyes lit up as he answered the question. "I first heard of Christ when I was on the ship coming to Europe."

"What do you mean 'first heard of'?" Ludwig asked. "St. Thomas has been ruled by European countries for many years. Surely you must have heard of Jesus Christ before then."

Anthony shook his head. "You do not understand," he replied, and then looking worried he added, "I did not mean to insult you."

"You did not," Ludwig assured him. "We are two brothers in Christ having a conversation. Feel free to share your observations. Tell me, how is it that you could live on a Christian island and not know about Christ Jesus?"

"Perhaps a story will help you understand, sir," Anthony replied. "When I was a child, a slave who was a coach driver drove his master to church. While the service was going on inside, the slave was expected to wait with the carriage. But this slave became curious. The church doors were closed, so he crept up to them and put his ear to the door to hear what was being said inside. Someone saw him and reported him to his master. Do you know what happened to him? The slave owner took out a knife and cut off his ears right there on the church steps."

Ludwig felt his stomach turn as he pictured such a gruesome act, on the steps of a church no less.

"You need to understand that the white people on Saint Thomas do not want their slaves to hear about Jesus Christ. They fear that the message will fill their heads with new ideas and cause them to rebel." Anthony then dropped his voice and added, "I wish that my brother and sister back on Saint Thomas could hear of the wonderful things I have learned about Jesus."

"What are their names?" Ludwig asked.

"Anna and Abraham," Anthony replied. "I feel sure they would embrace the gospel if only someone could share it with them."

"I shall make it a point to pray for them," Ludwig promised.

On the way home to Berthelsdorf, Ludwig could think of little else but the situation on Saint Thomas. Surely there had to be some way for the slaves on Saint Thomas to hear of Christ. It seemed unforgivable to him that white people would prevent their fellow human beings from hearing the most important message of all time. He was so glad that he had obtained permission from Count Laurwig for Anthony Ulrich to visit Herrnhut in a few days. Ludwig was sure that the hearts of many in the community would be stirred when they, too, heard Anthony's story.

On July 31, 1731, Ludwig and his traveling companions arrived back at Herrnhut. Even though he was tired from the long journey, Ludwig called a meeting of the community that night. He described for everyone his meeting with Anthony. Just as he had hoped, the plight of slaves on the islands of the Caribbean touched the hearts of many people in the community. Two days later Ludwig was holding a letter in his hand from two members of the single men's choir, Leonard Dober and Tobias Leupold. In the letter both men offered to go to Saint Thomas and share the gospel with Anthony's relatives and the other slaves there.

Four days after that, Anthony Ulrich arrived to tell his story. But much to Ludwig's surprise, Anthony was not pleased when he heard that Leonard and Tobias were ready to go to Saint Thomas. He warned that the slaves there were so embittered toward white people that they would not listen to anything the two young men had to say.

This was alarming news to Ludwig, who questioned Anthony to find out whether there was any way at all the slaves would listen to Leonard and Tobias. Anthony conceded that there might be one way to do it. The white missionaries would have to show that they were very different from the white slave owners. And the only way to show that would be if the missionaries were willing to live and work alongside the slaves, almost as slaves themselves. Perhaps then their message would be accepted.

It was a big challenge for Leonard and Tobias to consider living among the slaves, eating what they ate, and working alongside them. But Ludwig was proud when neither man shrank back from the challenge. Leonard declared to the Herrnhut community, "If it was good enough for the Lord Jesus to become a servant so that we might be saved, it is a worthy calling for us also. I leave it to the good judgement of the congregation, and have no other ground than this thought: that on the island there still are souls who cannot believe because they have not heard."

The response of Leonard and Tobias inspired two cousins, Matthäus Stach and Friedrich Bohnisch from the single men's choir, to offer themselves as missionaries as well. They wanted to go to Greenland because rumor suggested that Hans Egede, the missionary who had been appointed by the Danish royal court, was about to give up his mission work and return home. The cousins believed that they could carry on Hans's work.

These four young men were eager to begin their missionary endeavors, but the community at Herrnhut was not yet fully ready to send them. Most people in the community were suspicious of the whole idea of sending out missionaries. After all, no Protestant congregation had sent out missionaries since early Bible times. The few Protestants who had gone out as missionaries went under the patronage of a royal court, like the men from Halle who had gone to Tranquebar, India, and Hans Egede to Greenland.

Although Ludwig was eager for these young men to go, he decided it would be wise to wait until everyone was ready to send them.

In the meantime Erdmuth gave birth to another son, whom they named Johann. The baby was born on March 19, 1732, and died exactly two months later. He was Ludwig and Erdmuth's sixth child, of whom three were still alive.

In the midst of this personal tragedy, Ludwig watched his wife carry on with her many duties. By now Erdmuth was in charge of the family's finances, and since Ludwig provided much of the money for Herrnhut, she kept a close eye on what was happening there as well. It was a helpful arrangement for Ludwig, who was not interested in the details of ledgers and account books. In fact, he was so impressed with the way Erdmuth was handling the job that he signed over all of his estates to her. Erdmuth became the official owner of both Berthelsdorf and Herrnhut.

Ludwig signed everything over to his wife, partly because she was a better manager than he was and partly because he had a feeling that hard times lay ahead and the land would be safer in Erdmuth's name than in his own.

Finally, a little more than a year after Anthony Ulrich visited Herrnhut, the community agreed that they were willing to send missionaries to Saint Thomas. By now the leaders of the community were using the lot to determine many of their decisions, and during one of the community meetings they called Leonard Dober and Tobias Leupold to the front.

Ludwig watched closely as Tobias pulled from a small wooden box a tiny scroll with some words printed on it. As he read the scroll, his face fell, and he shook his head. "It is not God's will for me to go to Saint Thomas," he said. Next Leonard stepped forward. With a trembling hand he, too, picked a verse from the box. "Praise God, I am called!" he announced, walking over to Ludwig and handing him the scroll.

Ludwig read the words aloud. "Let the lad go, for the Lord is with him." He clasped Leonard's hand. "God will be your guide and your strength," he said.

Now the community looked around for someone who could accompany Leonard to Saint Thomas and help him to get established there. They chose David Nitschmann the carpenter and authorized him to stay with Leonard on Saint Thomas for the first four months. It did not take the two men long to pack, taking with them only a change of clothes, a sleeping mat, and a little food.

On August 18, 1732, the entire Herrnhut community gathered to commission the missionaries. They sang as they had never sung before, first twenty hymns, then forty, and then sixty. Still no one wanted to stop, and eventually over a hundred hymns were sung to speed Leonard and David on their way.

Two days later Ludwig needed to go to Dresden on business, and he offered to take the new missionaries as far as Bautzen, where the road forked to the west and to the north. The men left at three o'clock in the morning.

As the coach rattled along, Ludwig gave some last instructions to Leonard and David. "You must live among the people as one of them," he said. "Earn your own keep, for you are there to serve. Do not expect to convert masses of people at once. Remember, the Lord already knows those whose hearts He has prepared to believe. It is your job to find these people, even if they be few in number. They will be the precious 'firstfruits.'"

When they reached the fork in the road at Bautzen, Ludwig ordered the coachman to stop the carriage. The three men climbed out into the early-morning darkness. The two missionaries knelt together at the side of the road, and Ludwig prayed a prayer of blessing over them. "Let yourself always be led by the Spirit of Jesus Christ," was his last admonition to them before climbing back into his carriage.

Ludwig watched as the two determined young men took the fork in the road that headed north and soon disappeared into the darkness. He had given each man thirty shillings, though that was not nearly enough to pay for passage to Saint Thomas. The men would have the support of the twenty-four-hour prayer chain that was still continuing at Herrnhut, but they would have to find their own way to Saint Thomas, and they would be expected to earn their keep once they arrived there.

In the weeks that followed, Ludwig and the other members of the Herrnhut community waited expectantly for news from their new missionaries. Ludwig was more aware than anyone of the problems the two would face merely getting a ship to take them to Saint Thomas, so he was encouraged when he read their first letter to the community.

In the letter, dated October 8, 1732, Leonard explained just how much scoffing and ridicule he and David had faced so far. Most Christian people they met on the way to Copenhagen told them they were crazy and should return home. Only Countess von Stollberg at Wernigerode encouraged them. And when they reached Copenhagen, even the pious Christians within the royal court believed that they faced certain death if they went to Saint Thomas. They told the two missionaries that they would die either from some tropical disease or at the hand of a slave owner who did not take kindly to having someone preach to his slaves.

Leonard was glad, however, to report that their persistence had paid off. Slowly people's hearts began to change, and eventually some were willing to help them. Princess Charlotte Amelia gave them money and a Dutch Bible, as Dutch was the main language spoken on Saint Thomas. And since no Danish ship would transport them to the Caribbean, an officer in the royal court found a Dutch ship that was willing to take them on board as ship's carpenters. The officer of the court even convinced the ship's captain to buy the men their own set of carpenter's tools to use on the ship and which they could keep when they reached their destination.

All of this was heartening news to Ludwig, though it was followed soon afterward by the devastating death of yet another child. This time it was two-year-old Theodore. The only two Zinzendorf children who had survived the trials of childhood illnesses so far were six-year-old Benigna and five-year-old Christian Renatus. A seventh child, Christian Ludwig, was born on March 20, 1733.

Soon after the birth of his latest son, Ludwig received some terrible news. In 1726 he had allowed another persecuted religious group, the Schwenkfelders, to settle on the upper reaches of his Berthelsdorf estate when the group was expelled from neighboring Silesia. Now, on April 4, as Ludwig returned from a trip to Tübingen, he received word that a royal edict had been issued banishing the Schwenkfelders from Saxony. He was deeply troubled that this group would have to leave his estate. But what troubled Ludwig even more was the fact that if an edict could be so easily issued to banish one group of persecuted Christians from his land, a similar edict could just as easily be issued banning the Moravian refugees from Saxony. After all, the Moravians had come to Saxony seeking a safe haven from persecution just as the Schwenkfelders had.

As he rode along toward Berthelsdorf, Ludwig began to devise a plan of action in case the Moravians were ordered to leave Saxony. While he could not stop an edict from being issued, he could lessen the destructive impact it would have on the Herrnhut community. By the time Ludwig arrived at his estate, he had decided that he would divide Herrnhut into two groups, those who were German Lutherans and those who were refugees from Moravia. In this way, if the Moravians were ever banned from Saxony, they could move on without the Herrnhut community's collapsing. Ludwig also decided that the time was right for him to pursue becoming a Lutheran pastor. In this way he could deflect the criticism among religious leaders that the Lutherans at Herrnhut were not receiving proper pastoral oversight and were being overly influenced by the principles of the Unitas Fratrum.

When he arrived back at Berthelsdorf, a group of leaders from the Schwenkfelders approached Ludwig and asked for his help. They had heard of General James Oglethorpe and his plan to let people fleeing religious persecution into his Georgia colony in North America. They wanted Ludwig to intercede on their behalf and secure a new home for them in Georgia. Ludwig did as he was asked and obtained permission for them all to emigrate to Georgia, where they would be granted land to live on.

Still, the news of the Schwenkfelders' banishment did not dim Ludwig's or the Herrnhut community's newfound zeal for missions. On April 17, 1733, David Nitschmann the carpenter arrived back at Herrnhut, and Ludwig was eager to learn from him how things were progressing in Saint Thomas. The day after his arrival, David and Ludwig went for a stroll together on the Berthelsdorf estate. "Tell me all about Saint Thomas," Ludwig said.

"We arrived on the island on December 13. I wish I had the words to describe it adequately. It was so different from anything I had ever seen before. Lush green hills and beaches that sparkled in the noonday sun. And palm trees lined the shore. It was hard to imagine that in such a beautiful place so many did not know of the Savior. We walked along the narrow streets of Tappus looking for lodging, and it was there that we came upon Mr. Lorenzen, a planter on the island. Mr. Lorenzen proved to be God's answer to our prayers. He offered us free lodging until such time as we were able to earn money to pay our own way. I soon began plying my trade as a carpenter to earn the money we needed."

Ludwig nodded. "So it was possible to earn your own keep?"

"For me, yes," David replied. "But it was not possible for Leonard. We looked long and hard, but we could not find any clay for him to make his pots with."

"Interesting," Ludwig interjected. "Continue with your report."

"On our first Sunday on Saint Thomas, we went in search of Abraham and Anna, Anthony's brother and sister, so that we might deliver the letter Anthony had given us for them. We found them and read the letter aloud. In it Anthony told of his conversion to Christianity and pleaded for his siblings to do the same. We then explained salvation to Abraham and Anna. Soon other black slaves gathered round to listen. They were astonished to learn that we wanted to tell them about God. Until that point they were barred from listening to any Bible readings or preaching. But their hearts did not soften right away. They remained wary of us, fearing that our appearance among them was some trick of their masters. At times they tried to chase us away. But we prayed and persisted in our efforts to share the gospel with them.

"In April I boarded a ship to return home. Before I left, I prayed fervently that God would watch over and encourage Leonard. The work ahead is hard. Not only do the slaves remain suspicious of us, but also most often the slave owners treat us with contempt and hatred for our work. We must all pray that God will guide Leonard to those firstfruits you spoke of upon our departure."

Ludwig was both excited and saddened by David's report. He was excited that they had made it safely to Saint Thomas and had begun their missionary work, but the task of winning converts was going to be every bit as difficult as Anthony had told them. Yet he believed that in time God would indeed guide Leonard to the firstfruits.

Within days of David's arrival back at Herrnhut, Matthäus Stach and his brother Christian, along with Christian David, left the community bound for Greenland, with Friedrich Bohnisch following a year later. There, like Leonard on Saint Thomas, they would face many challenges, from the difficult language they needed to learn to hostile Eskimos who thought they had come to steal from them. With the sending of these first missionaries to Saint Thomas and Greenland, while the Moravians were still praying for the firstfruits, something beyond even Ludwig's imagination had begun.

Chapter 9

# The Expanding Work

Although a lot of government suspicion had been aroused regarding Herrnhut, the community continued to thrive, with more Christians continuing to arrive from all over Germany and beyond. One of these new arrivals at Herrnhut would prove to be a loyal friend and helper to Ludwig. He was twenty-nine-year-old August Gottlieb Spangenberg, a brilliant scholar who had recently earned a master's degree from the University of Jena. On a trip through Jena, Ludwig had met August and immediately liked him. August was a good-natured and genuine man and was one of the leading Pietists at the university. He also had a habit of putting his faith into action, and in Jena he had helped found several free schools for poor children.

In late spring 1733 August decided to join the Herrnhut community. Ludwig was delighted with August's decision, and soon after his arrival at Herrnhut, August became Ludwig's personal assistant. Like Erdmuth, he handled many of the daily details of Ludwig's life as well as of the Herrnhut community.

In December 1733 Ludwig asked August to accompany Tobias Leupold, along with fourteen men and four women, as far as Copenhagen. The group was bound for Saint Thomas and the nearby island of Saint Croix. Tobias was to replace Leonard on Saint Thomas. While absent, Leonard had been voted the new chief elder of the community and needed to return to Herrnhut as soon as possible.

Another large meeting was held to commission the new missionaries and send them on their way. During the service Ludwig spoke from his heart, instructing the missionaries. "Remember," he said, "you must never use your position to lord it over the heathen. Instead you must humble yourself and earn their respect through your own quiet faith and the power of the Holy Spirit. The missionary must seek nothing for himself, no seat of honor or hope of fame. Like the cabhorse in London, each of you must wear blinkers that blind you to every danger and to every snare and conceit. You must be content to suffer, to die, and to be forgotten."

While he waited for Leonard to return and take up his new position, Ludwig appointed eighteen-year-old Anna Nitschmann to fill in as chief elder.

Anna had more than proved her worth and her faith as head of the single women's choir.

A short time after the departure of the missionaries for Saint Thomas and Saint Croix, another group left the Berthelsdorf estate. Ludwig sadly said good-bye to the Schwenkfelders, who were on their way to Holland, from where they planned to sail to North America.

With the group of missionaries safely on their way to the Caribbean, Ludwig set about fulfilling his plan of becoming a Lutheran pastor. He dared not tell his mother what he was up to. He knew she would be horrified that her son, a count, was willing to stoop to become a pastor. Of course he knew that word would eventually get back to her, but he would wait until then to discuss the matter with her.

On his return from Copenhagen, August helped Ludwig to study and prepare for the rigorous process of ordination. In April 1734 Ludwig felt ready to travel to Stralsund for his first set of examinations. The exams, which were conducted in both German and Latin, lasted for three days. At the end of the examinations, Ludwig was required to preach a series of five sermons.

Much to his delight, Ludwig passed all the examinations and the preaching test and was given a certificate of orthodoxy. This meant that he was now able to apply to become a Lutheran pastor, though this next step required a lot of patience on his part, as he needed to have an exception made for him. Normally, before he could be ordained, a Lutheran pastor had to name the Lutheran congregation that had called him. But Ludwig had no congregation to call him. The people he wanted to minister to were the Christians at Herrnhut, and they were not a recognized Lutheran congregation. Ludwig began writing letters to influential church and state leaders, hoping to find a way around the situation.

Meanwhile Erdmuth gave birth to an eighth child. Their second daughter, whom they named Anna, was born on August 7, 1734. The following month, Leonard finally arrived back at Herrnhut from Saint Thomas. With him he had a seven-year-old black boy named Oly.

Soon after his arrival, a meeting was held so that Leonard could report to the community on his missionary work on Saint Thomas. The atmosphere in the room was electric as Leonard stood to speak. Everyone first wanted to know about Oly.

"Oly is the firstfruit of the work on Saint Thomas," Leonard began.

Ludwig watched with delight as a broad smile spread across Oly's face at these words.

"Soon after Brother David left Saint Thomas to return here to Herrnhut, Oly befriended me. He is an orphan boy, and his company cheered me through many lonely times. Together we played and laughed, and slowly I told him about the Savior's love. At first he did not seem interested, but then one day after many months, Oly told me that he now wanted to believe in God and become a Christian. Of course I was delighted and wept with joy at his decision.

He was the first, but he will not be the last. Others will follow his lead."

Ludwig listened carefully to all that Leonard had to say. The work of proclaiming the gospel in foreign lands was difficult, but bit by bit it was moving forward.

While everyone sat spellbound, Leonard went on to tell how he had taken care of many black slaves who were sick with malaria. Most of them had died, but the other slaves noticed Leonard's selflessness in ministering to those who became sick. When a slave revolt broke out on the nearby island of Saint John, every white man except one was killed. The white slave owners on Saint Thomas feared that the rebellion would spread to their island and that the slaves would rise up and kill them. They ordered all whites off the plantations for their own safety, but Leonard refused to leave. He explained that God had called him to minister to the slaves, and if he was killed in the course of doing that, he was ready to die.

Thankfully the revolt did not spread to Saint Thomas, and eventually French troops were brought in to quell the rebellion on Saint John, but not before several hundred slaves had been killed.

It wasn't the slave rebellion, however, that nearly claimed Leonard's life; rather it was malaria. Leonard had become sick before Christmas and had spent days lying on his bed, hovering between life and death. When he finally recovered, he abandoned trying to make a living as a potter. There was virtually no suitable clay on the island to fashion into pots.

Instead Leonard took a job as a night watchman to earn his keep. All in all, Leonard summed up his time on Saint Thomas as both challenging and rewarding. God had blessed him and blessed others through him.

Following Leonard's report on the progress of missionary work on Saint Thomas, many others in the community were stirred to offer themselves for service overseas. Ludwig could not have been happier. The following month, however, Ludwig received a letter from Tobias Leupold, informing him that nine of the nineteen missionaries who had gone to Saint Thomas and Saint Croix were dead from malaria and other tropical diseases.

The news from Greenland was just as discouraging. A fierce epidemic of smallpox had broken out on the island's west coast and had killed more than three thousand people. Although the missionaries were working tirelessly among the native people, no one had yet responded to their message. The smallpox had been carried into the villages by an Eskimo who had visited Europe, causing many in Greenland to question the value of having anything to do with the outside world.

Still, Ludwig was encouraged to hear that the three missionaries in Greenland had made a covenant among themselves. They had promised to "never forget that we have come here resting upon Christ our Savior, in whom all the nations of the earth shall be blessed, not on the principle of sight but of faith."

Despite the setbacks, the members of the Herrnhut community had by now thoroughly embraced Ludwig's vision of preaching the gospel in foreign lands. More and more members stepped forward to offer themselves for missionary service in various parts of the world. Soon missionaries were preparing to set out to work in Surinam and Lapland.

While all of this was going on, Ludwig was still trying to find a way to reach his goal of becoming a Lutheran pastor. Every door he tried was shut in his face, until August Spangenberg interceded on his behalf with the faculty of the university in Tübingen. Finally the faculty agreed that their church laws did allow for a pastor to become fully ordained without his being assigned to a specific congregation. This finding opened the way for Ludwig, and soon afterward the Lutheran Church granted him permission to become a pastor without a parish. In early December 1734, Ludwig traveled to Tübingen to be ordained.

As part of his ordination requirements, Ludwig had to write out his testimony. He thought for a long time about how to condense so much information into a few paragraphs. Eventually he wrote:

> I was but ten years old when I began to direct my companions to Jesus, as their Redeemer. My deficiency of knowledge was compensated by sincerity. Now I am thirty-four; and though I have made various experiences, yet in the main my mind has undergone no change. My zeal is not cooled.... I will continue as

> heretofore, to win souls for my precious Savior, to gather His sheep, bid guests, and hire servants for Him.... I shall go to distant nations, who are ignorant of Jesus and of redemption in His blood. I shall endeavor to imitate the labors of my brethren, who have the honor of being the first messengers to the heathen.... The love of Christ shall constrain me, and His cross refresh me. I will cheerfully be subject to the higher powers, and a sincere friend to my enemies.

On December 19, 1734, Count Ludwig von Zinzendorf was officially ordained as a pastor in the Lutheran Church. His ordination was the fulfillment of a dream and a way to protect the community he loved. Now he could shelter the Herrnhut community from accusations of being anti-Lutheran. He could also perform all of the offices of a state-appointed minister, baptizing, marrying, burying, and serving communion.

In the meantime, August Spangenberg had made a trip to London to meet with General James Oglethorpe and James Vernon, the secretary of the trustees of the Georgia colony in North America. There he was able to secure a land grant in the colony of five hundred acres along the Ogeechee River. In early 1735 August led a group of nine Moravian missionaries from Herrnhut to Georgia. Their purpose for going was twofold. First, the Moravians in Georgia could prepare a place for their brethren at Herrnhut to flee to in case they were banished from Saxony, and second, it provided them with a base from which they could launch missionary work among the Indians of North America.

The year 1735 continued to be a time of sending out more missionaries. In January two men set out for the Guinea coast of Africa, and in May, eleven more missionaries arrived on Saint Croix.

Word reached Herrnhut later that year that Tobias Leupold had died, as had seven of the newly arrived missionaries. And nine other missionaries, including some of those who had originally gone out with Tobias, were so weakened physically that they decided to return to Herrnhut for rest. Three of them died on the journey home. All in all, twenty-two of the first twenty-nine missionaries sent out were dead. The Herrnhut community dubbed the sad situation "The Great Dying." Some observers expected them to give up their mission work in light of the great cost of human lives, but just the opposite happened. For every missionary who died, two stepped up to take his or her place. A mission was opened in Surinam, on the northeast coast of South America, and zealous missionaries set out to staff it, knowing that their chances of ever seeing their families and homeland again were slim.

Although Ludwig was concerned that the Moravian refugees at Herrnhut might be banished from Saxony, to his surprise, it was he who was banished from the kingdom! Resentment toward his unorthodox religious ways had been growing among the nobility in Saxony for some time. And many thought he had gone too far when he, a count, was ordained a Lutheran pastor. Such an act upset the religious and social ideals that kept people in their "proper place." Eventually Baron Huldenberg of Neukirch, a Saxon nobleman, could take it no longer. He complained to the royal court in Dresden that Ludwig was enticing people who lived on his estate to come and live at Herrnhut. For the royal court it was one complaint too many against Ludwig, and on March 20, 1736, the new Saxon monarch, King Frederick Augustus III, issued an edict banning him from the kingdom.

It was not until April 21, as Ludwig was making his way home after a trip to Holland with Erdmuth, their children, and a group from the Herrnhut community, that he heard the news. Instead of returning to the estate in Berthelsdorf, the group made its way to Ebersdorf, where Ludwig could stay with friends until he worked out what to do next.

As shocking as this new development was, Ludwig refused to let his banishment from Saxony destroy him or his work. Instead, he saw it as God's opportunity to expand his work far beyond Berthelsdorf. He began searching for a new place to live. As he looked, he heard about two medieval castles named Ronneburg and Marienborn, located in the district of Wetteravia. The two castles were run-down and unoccupied and sat on the estate of Count Casimir of Büdingen. The count had fallen on hard times financially, and Ludwig learned that he would be willing to lease them to him.

Ludwig sent Christian David, recently returned from Greenland, to check out Ronneburg castle. Christian's report was not good. Ronneburg castle was decayed and filthy and definitely no place for a count of the Holy Roman Empire to live. To make matters worse, the castle outhouses, farms, and stables were let out to fifty-six families of Jews, tramps, and "vagabonds" of the lowest order. Christian encouraged Ludwig to look elsewhere for a place to live.

As he listened carefully to Christian's report, Ludwig could not shake the feeling that as bleak as the castle sounded, this was the place God had chosen for the extension of his work. *Why not start working among the lowest class of men?* Ludwig wondered. *Surely the gospel was for them as much as for anyone else.* He told Christian about his decision, saying, "I will make the place and the nest of vagabonds you speak of the center for the universal religion of the Savior."

Christian did everything he could to dissuade Ludwig from living in such a vile place, but Ludwig had made up his mind. If that was the place God had chosen for them, they could go nowhere else.

Within days Ludwig had agreed to terms with Count Casimir of Büdingen to lease Ronneburg castle, and soon he and the group from Herrnhut traveling with him moved in. On June 17, 1736, Ludwig preached his first sermon in the castle.

As Christian had reported, Ronneburg castle was indeed run-down. The walls were crumbling in places, the roof leaked, and when the sun went down, the castle became an eerie place. Rats and mice scurried up and down the rotting staircases, and the wind howled in through the broken windows. The castle had little usable furniture, and everyone, including Ludwig and Erdmuth and the children, slept on a pile of straw on the floor. *Despite the living conditions, Ludwig encouraged the small group with him to turn the place into a home. They began clearing away the piles of rotting wood and scrubbing down the walls.

Within days the group opened a free school for the "vagabond" children, teaching both the boys and the girls to read and write. They also held Christian meetings for the adults and visited people in their tumbling-down homes. Soon the children were being invited to the castle to eat with Ludwig's children. It was a strange sight to all to see wretchedly poor children in tattered clothes eating with the noble children of a count.

Ludwig also issued an order forbidding begging. Instead, twice a week he arranged for food and clothing to be distributed to the poor who lived around the castle.

One day, as he was taking a walk around the grounds of the castle, Ludwig met a gray-haired Jewish man named Rabbi Abraham. As soon as the old rabbi saw Ludwig, he started to shuffle away. Ludwig stopped him. "Stay and talk with me," he said kindly. "Gray hairs are a crown of glory. I can see from your head and the expression in your eyes that you have had much experience both of heart and of life. In the name of the God of Abraham, Isaac, and Jacob, let us be friends." He stretched out his hand to shake Rabbi Abraham's.

The old man just stood staring, his mouth wide open.

"I sense your discomfort," Ludwig said. "I am sure you have probably not heard such a greeting from a Christian before. Most likely they have greeted you with words like, 'Begone, Jew!'"

Rabbi Abraham's lips began to tremble, and tears formed in his eyes.

"Enough, father," Ludwig said, comfortingly. "We worship the same God, and we understand each other. What stops us from being friends?"

From then on the two became friends. Ludwig regularly visited Rabbi Abraham in his small, rundown home, and many times they would take walks together early in the morning before the sun rose.

One morning, as the two men walked in the predawn darkness, Rabbi Abraham opened his heart to Ludwig. "My heart longs for the dawn," he said. "I am sick, yet I don't know what is the matter with me. I am looking for something, yet I don't know what I seek. I am like one who is chased, yet I see no enemy, except the one within me, my old evil heart."

Seizing the opportunity, Ludwig began to share the gospel with Rabbi Abraham. He told him about Jesus, how He had become a man so that He might bring men back to God, and how He was put to death on the cross. As Ludwig spoke, tears began to run down Rabbi Abraham's cheeks and dripped onto his long, gray beard.

The two men climbed a low hill, on top of which stood a small church. As the sun rose, the golden cross on the church spire glistened in its rays.

"See there, Rabbi Abraham," Ludwig said. "It is a sign from heaven for you. The God of your fathers has placed the cross in your sight, and now the rising sun has tinged it with heavenly splendor. Believe on Him whose blood was shed by your fathers, that God's purpose of mercy might be fulfilled, that you might be free from all sin and find in Him your salvation."

"So be it," Rabbi Abraham said. "Blessed be the Lord who has had mercy on me."

Ludwig was delighted by Rabbi Abraham's decision to become a Christian. God was already beginning to bless the new community, which they had decided would be called Herrnhaag, after the Haag Church located nearby.

On November 6, 1736, Ludwig received another blessing. Erdmuth gave birth to a daughter they named Maria.

As the Herrnhaag community grew, Ludwig began inviting the people there to become part of a "Pilgrim Band." He saw them as a sort of traveling church—a band of Christians called to "proclaim the Savior to the world." His new motto became "The earth is the Lord's; all souls are His; I am debtor to all." He saw that this debt was repaid by both proclaiming the gospel to the people of the world and seeing that the unity among Christians was strengthened wherever he went. And since he was banned from returning to Berthelsdorf and Saxony, he intended to go to as many places as he could with the message of hope.

Chapter 10

# A Great Sermon to Us

The year 1737 began with terrible news. Ludwig wept openly when he heard that the authorities in Russia had turned back three missionaries from Herrnhut who had gone to work with the Samoyede people living along the shore of the Arctic Ocean. The authorities warned the men that if they ever showed their faces in Russia again, they would be burned at the stake.

Then on August 31 that same year, three-year-old Christian Ludwig von Zinzendorf died of a fever. Again Ludwig found himself weeping openly.

Amidst the despair, however, good things were happening. Ludwig received an exciting account from August Spangenberg. August reported that the group from Herrnhut had made many friends while aboard the *Simmonds* on their way to Georgia. In London the ship had picked up General James Oglethorpe, the governor of the Georgia colony. Traveling with him was his secretary Charles Wesley, whose brother John was also on board. John was on his way to Georgia to work as an Anglican missionary. August wrote that he and John had enjoyed many enriching conversations together. John was very interested in the way the members of the Herrnhut community lived out their faith.

The following year Ludwig found himself in London, where he rented rooms for six weeks at Lindsey House in Chelsea. He had gone to London to talk about future plans for more Moravians to emigrate to Georgia. By then Charles Wesley had returned from America, and he was the man Ludwig dealt with on behalf of the Georgia colony.

Charles and Ludwig became friends almost immediately. Although Ludwig spoke limited English, the two men spent hours together speaking in Latin. They would often meet together at Lindsey House to pray and sing hymns. Charles introduced Ludwig to many Pietistic English men and women, and Ludwig enjoyed his fellowship with these like-minded Christians. It was also in England that people began referring to the Unitas Fratrum and the Herrnhut and Herrnhaag communities as the Moravian Church, and the name began to stick.

Soon after his return from England, Ludwig was ordained as a bishop in the Moravian Church. This did not mean that he gave up being a Lutheran pastor. Rather, Ludwig had the unique position of holding office in two denominations at the same time. He became a bishop in the church because he needed to be able to ordain other ministers among the Moravians. Many of the missionaries who had been sent out from Herrnhut were having difficulty because they were not ordained. They were forbidden to perform many pastoral tasks, such as conducting weddings, baptizing converts, and serving communion. Yet if they did not do these things, who would? In many instances, white traders, slave owners, and government officials blocked slaves and natives from attending the Moravians' churches.

Some people thought that Ludwig had changed from being a Lutheran to being a Moravian, but the truth was that he had little time for people who concerned themselves too much about what denomination a Christian belonged to.

"Is not the greatest unity to agree that souls think differently?" one Moravian asked Ludwig.

"Yes," Ludwig replied. "That is the real bond of unity. Nature is full of different creatures of different inclinations, and it is the same in the spiritual world. We must learn to regard various ways of thinking as something beautiful. There are as many religious ideas as there are believing souls, so we cannot force everyone to measure up to the same yardstick. Only God, according to His infinite wisdom, knows how to deal with every soul."

As life in exile progressed for Ludwig, the elders

at Herrnhut wrote to him regularly and often visited Herrnhaag. Meanwhile, Erdmuth produced a tenth and then an eleventh child. Johanna was born August 4, 1737, and David, on October 22, 1738. Two months after David's arrival, four-year-old Anna died. She was buried in God's Acre, the community cemetery at Herrnhaag.

With the expansion of the Unitas Fratrum community, the missionary work continued to expand. Soon George Schmidt volunteered to go to work among the Hottentot tribe in South Africa. Although the Dutch East India Company had ruled South Africa for one hundred years, it had done nothing to share Christianity with the Hottentots. In fact, quite the opposite was true. The Dutch clergymen in South Africa referred to the Hottentots as "black cattle" and preached that they had no souls and belonged to a race of baboons. All of this touched the hearts and consciences of the Moravians, who gladly sent George off to work among their black brothers.

Other Moravian missionaries went to Amsterdam, Holland, where they worked among Jewish people. This was something very new. To this point most Christian denominations viewed the Jews with suspicion and often with contempt. But now here was a group who had come just to focus on sharing the gospel with the Jews. In going to the Jews in this way, they were following Ludwig's example with Rabbi Abraham.

Exciting news from Greenland also arrived. After an unpromising start to the missionary work there, in June 1738 a "great awakening" had broken out in

Greenland. Many people were becoming Christians and were being added to the church.

Ludwig rejoiced when he heard of all the good things that were happening. He prayed and fasted more fervently for all those missionaries who were in difficult situations. Still some people criticized him. "The count is willing to send others to die of diseases on foreign soil, but he is not willing to go himself!" they said.

Such comments challenged Ludwig, who began to wonder whether indeed he should go to the mission field himself, perhaps to Saint Thomas, where the Moravian missionary effort had begun. Ludwig wrestled with the idea, but he could find no peace about what to do. Finally he decided to use the lot to see whether or not he should make a trip to Saint Thomas. He prayed, reached into the small, wooden box, and pulled out a scroll of paper. According to the lot, God was directing him to Saint Thomas.

Ludwig began putting his affairs in order. He drew up a last will and testament and published what he titled his last sermon. He did this because he fully expected to die while on Saint Thomas. So many Moravian missionaries had already died there that Ludwig found it difficult to think he would meet a different fate. He told people before he left, "I have been commissioned by the Lord God to spread the word of Jesus without concern as to what happens to me as a result."

In November 1738 Ludwig, accompanied by George Weber and several other Moravians, set sail for the Caribbean islands. The wind on the journey was favorable, and passage across the Atlantic Ocean was swift. As the sailing ship carrying the group gently pitched back and forth, running before the wind, Ludwig thought about what he would find when he arrived at Saint Thomas. Following the death of Tobias Leupold, Friedrich Martin had taken over the mission work on Saint Thomas. He had been joined a few months later by Matthäus Freundlich, who was the last survivor of the group of missionaries who had gone to Saint Croix. Ludwig had read some good reports of their work on Saint Thomas. August Spangenberg had made a trip there two years before and had written telling Ludwig how the number of Christian converts there was still small but growing. August had even had the pleasure of baptizing several of the new converts while there.

The cost of the work on the islands had been high. Many Moravian missionaries had died on both Saint Thomas and nearby Saint Croix. Yellow fever and other tropical diseases were still a constant threat, striking a healthy and strong man or woman down in a matter of a few days.

As the lush, green hills of Saint Thomas appeared on the horizon, Ludwig finally voiced his thoughts and concerns to George Weber. "What if we find no one there? What if the missionaries are all dead?" he said, motioning toward Saint Thomas with his head.

"Then *we* are here," George replied confidently.

"You are an indestructible race, you Moravians," Ludwig exclaimed to his traveling companion, as he clapped him on the back. "I marvel at you!"

It was true. The Moravians never ceased to amaze Ludwig with their determination, no matter what the cost, to go throughout the world and proclaim the gospel. And here on Saint Thomas, if all of the missionaries previously sent out were dead, George and the other Moravians on board were ready to pick up where their brethren had left off.

It was a clear, sunny day on Thursday, January 29, 1739, when Ludwig finally stepped ashore on Saint Thomas. As he walked through the streets of Tappus, the main community on the island, he was eager to make contact with Friedrich Martin and Matthäus Freundlich. "Do you know where the Moravian brethren are?" he asked a slave he came upon just outside of town. "Are they alive?"

"They are alive," the slave said.

Ludwig said a quick prayer of thanks. "Where are they?" he asked.

"In prison," the slave replied.

Ludwig took a moment to digest what he had just heard. "How long have they been there?" he asked.

"For over three months," came the reply.

"This is an outrage," Ludwig snapped. "They have permission from the Danish authorities to preach to the people. How dare anyone throw them in prison!" It was then that he noticed that the slave was smiling. "What can make you happy about missionaries being imprisoned?" he asked.

"The imprisonment of the missionaries is a great sermon to us," the slave declared. "I myself have come to accept their message as a result of it. We slaves are astonished to see that our masters treat the missionaries in the same manner they treat us. We have come to understand that the missionaries are not like the slave owners. No, they are our friends, willing to suffer for us."

The slave grinned widely, and Ludwig noticed the sparkle in his eyes. "A great revival is beginning. You should be happy the missionaries have been in prison, for their influence has grown widely among the slaves as a result."

"Your observation is correct. God has obviously allowed a great wrong to be turned to good for His sake. But now we must see what can be done about the situation," Ludwig said.

Ludwig soon learned that a Reformed clergyman on Saint Thomas had complained to the island governor that the Moravian missionaries had baptized some of their converts without an ordained minister being present. This was not true. In fact, Friedrich Martin had been ordained through a letter from the Moravians at Herrnhut. But the Reformed pastor refused to accept this ordination and continued to complain to the governor, who eventually had the Moravian missionaries locked up.

When he learned all the details, Ludwig marched in to see the governor. He burst into his mansion like a thunderbolt, demanding the missionaries be released from jail. The startled governor did not seem to know quite what to do. It was not wise to antagonize a European count, but on the other hand, he did not want to make church leaders on the island angry with him.

Ludwig showed the governor a document signed by the king of Denmark and authorizing the Moravians to preach in the Danish West Indies. The governor had no option. He issued an order that the prisoners be immediately released. Once and for all, the document put the work of the Moravians on Saint Thomas on solid legal ground.

Friedrich and Matthäus were both delighted to be out of prison and to see Ludwig in person on Saint Thomas. They all retreated to the small plantation the Moravians had bought a year before as a base for their mission work. Ludwig called the place Posaunenberg (Trumpet Mount) when he saw it.

After he had been on the island several days, Ludwig was so impressed by the work the missionaries had done that he wrote in his diary, "Saint Thomas is a greater marvel than Herrnhut."

In many ways it was. For three years Friedrich had worked tirelessly building the work of the Moravians on Saint Thomas. Despite fierce opposition from planters and other religious leaders, he had managed to establish several native congregations. He had also set up a school for slave boys and formed the new converts into societies for Bible study and prayer.

Ludwig was eager to see the work progress further, so he set up a single men's and a single women's choir and appointed leaders for each. And as at Herrnhut, he established helpers for the community, along with advisers and distributors of alms. He also introduced the system of twenty-four-hour prayer that still continued at Herrnhut.

In the evenings Ludwig preached at Posaunenberg, where up to six hundred slaves at a time came to hear him. With each passing night, Ludwig's excitement grew. The slave man he had spoken with upon his arrival on Saint Thomas had been right: a revival was beginning on the island.

Finally Ludwig's time on Saint Thomas drew to a close. On his last night on the island, eight hundred people came to hear him speak. He had a surprise for them. Ludwig always encouraged missionaries to learn the local language as quickly as possible, and he tried to follow his own advice. During his stay he had made a real effort to learn the dialect of the slaves. When he rose to preach that night, he spoke to the slaves in Dutch Creole. The slaves were greatly moved, and many became Christians as a result of Ludwig's preaching that night.

Ludwig also made short visits to encourage the Moravians on the neighboring islands of Saint Croix and Saint John before boarding a ship for the return voyage to Europe. Despite his worst fears, he had not died in this part of the world. The sermon he had published before he left, titled "Count Zinzendorf's Last Sermon," would have to be given a new name. As the ship cut through the waters of the Atlantic Ocean, Ludwig thanked God for preserving his health, glad to know that he would soon be back in the company of his wife and children.

Chapter 11

# Bethlehem

Ludwig returned to Europe and continued to travel, encouraging Christians wherever he went. But the trip to Saint Thomas had fired even more his passion for missions, and he looked forward to the prospect of going overseas again. By now more than seventy Moravians had gone out to the mission field. Some had gone to support existing mission bases, while others had gone to establish new bases in Ceylon, Romania, Algeria, and Constantinople. Everywhere the mission work of the Moravians was growing.

The impetus Ludwig needed to go again to the mission field came as the result of a letter from August Spangenberg, now in Pennsylvania.

The Moravian missionaries who had emigrated to Georgia had struggled since arriving in the colony. Their numbers had dwindled from thirty to twelve and then to six. Many had died, and others had returned to Herrnhut, discouraged and ill. To make matters worse, the Spanish army, stationed in Florida, was preparing to invade Georgia from the south and claim it for Spain. The governor of Georgia had called for all colonists to buy guns and prepare to defend their colony. But the Moravians had refused to do this. They would not kill others in the name of political and geographical ambition.

The Moravians' position did not sit well with the leaders of Georgia, and the matter soon came to a head. The Moravians were ordered to either bear arms or leave the colony. At that time a fiery evangelist named George Whitefield was preaching in Savannah. When he heard of the plight of the remaining Moravians in Georgia, he offered them free passage on his ship bound for Pennsylvania. He also offered them work there building a school for Indian children on a tract of land he had recently purchased and named Nazareth. Thus, the center for Moravian missions in North America moved from Georgia to Pennsylvania.

It was not the mission itself, however, that tugged at Ludwig's heart the most, but the news that the one hundred thousand or so Germans who had settled in Pennsylvania were in spiritual trouble. Many of these people had fled to William Penn's colony to escape religious persecution in the various German kingdoms. But virtually no pastors or church leaders were around to watch over their spiritual needs. As a result, the people had begun to splinter into many small church groupings and sects with such names as Dunkers, Mennonites, French Prophets, Freethinkers, Hermits, Newborn Ones, New-lights, Protestant Monks and Nuns, Independents, Separatists, and Calvinists. Reports back to Europe suggested that they spent most of their time and energy criticizing one another. No one thought of banding together to reach the nearby Indians with the gospel. August also pointed out that almost all of these people spoke only German, meaning that they could not worship with non-German Christian settlers.

Ludwig felt moved to help these settlers get along with one another and get on with the task of spreading the gospel among the Indians. He gathered a group of seven "pilgrims," including his fifteen-year-old daughter Benigna, and set out for North America. Erdmuth stayed behind at Herrnhaag because her expertise was needed to keep the financial affairs of the Moravian Church on track. She also had another baby, their twelfth child, to look after. The baby, whose name was Elisabeth, had been born on April 25, 1740.

Ludwig and his pilgrim band arrived in New York City on November 29, 1741. They stayed there a week, meeting with the governor of the colony and other city officials. From New York they made their way overland to Philadelphia, where, as in New York, Ludwig met with the governor of the colony and other important people, including Benjamin Franklin.

While aboard ship, crossing the Atlantic Ocean, Ludwig had decided that he would not be called Count Zinzendorf in Pennsylvania. Too many Germans and other Europeans had fled to North America to get away from rigid social structures, and insisting on being addressed as Count could well serve to antagonize them. Besides, he was not coming to America as a German nobleman but as a fellow Christian. Instead of being addressed as Count Zinzendorf, Ludwig decided he would be known as Herr Louis von Thurnstein, Thurnstein being an old family title. The Quakers of Pennsylvania were soon referring to him as Friend Louis.

The Moravians in Pennsylvania were now led by David Nitschmann the carpenter, who had been ordained a bishop in the church. Under his leadership they had purchased five hundred acres of land at the junction of the Lehigh River and the Monocacy Creek. There the Moravians had already erected their first log meetinghouse and several homes. The land was located about fifty miles northwest of Philadelphia, deep in what was known as Indian country, and was a perfect base for ministering to the Indians.

It took Ludwig and Benigna and the others ten days to reach the new Moravian settlement, where a warm welcome awaited them. Ludwig was greatly impressed with the undaunted courage these Moravians showed living deep in the wilderness. The people had set up simple homes and had already gone out among the Indian tribes to share the gospel with them.

Two days later, on Christmas Eve, Ludwig preached to the group in the newly erected meeting-house. It was during this sermon that he announced that the new settlement would be called Bethlehem, Pennsylvania, in honor of Jesus' birthplace.

Right after the new year, Ludwig set out from Bethlehem for Germantown, where he met with a man named Henry Antes. Even though Henry was not a Moravian, he too was deeply troubled by the lack of churches, pastors, and schools in Pennsylvania. He and Ludwig discussed the problem and decided to call a meeting, or synod, as they called it, of all the Christian denominations in the colony. On January 12, 1742, over one hundred people showed up to listen to Ludwig speak to them on laying aside their dislike for one another and working together for everyone's benefit.

This was just the kind of work Ludwig had come to America to do, and the task energized him. He traveled the length and breadth of Pennsylvania, talking to all kinds of men and women about their church experiences and what could be done to bring Christians together.

Meanwhile Ludwig's daughter Benigna set about opening the first boarding school for girls in America, and soon a thriving school was situated at Bethlehem.

More synods were held to discuss the future of the denominations in Pennsylvania. However, the Pennsylvania Germans began to argue and fight among themselves at these meetings. Some of them ended up hating each other more than they had before the synods took place. This was a disappointing outcome for Ludwig, who had hoped that these men and women of Pennsylvania who had been given the wonderful gift of religious freedom would use it wisely.

Still, Ludwig pressed on. A local band of Lutherans in Philadelphia who met in a barn on Arch Street invited him to be their pastor. They had not had a pastor for five years, mainly because they could not afford to support one. Ludwig accepted the position, not only working for free but paying for a permanent church to be built on Race Street. In addition, he preached at the nearby Reformed Church, which also did not have a pastor.

Once Ludwig could see that his plan for one united German church in Pennsylvania was not going to work out, he focused his attention on reaching out to the Indians. To do this, he and the other Moravian elders came up with a unique plan. They would convert the settlement at Bethlehem into a large missionary-sending center. Everyone in the settlement would be assigned one of two roles: he or she either would be a missionary/teacher or would dedicate himself or herself to supporting the missionary work with his or her time and money.

The 120 people who were now living at Bethlehem heartily agreed with the plan, and soon bands of men and women were preparing to travel deep into Indian country. One Moravian missionary,

Christian Henry Rauch, had already gone out from Bethlehem to the Indians, and one evening he walked back into the settlement accompanied by an Indian man. Christian Henry introduced the Indian as Tschoop, and soon Tschoop and Ludwig were deep in conversation.

"Christian Henry tells me that you are a believer in Christ," Ludwig began.

"Yes, I am," Tschoop said, his eyes blazing with zeal.

"Tell me, brother, how did that come to be?"

Tschoop leaned back on his chair and folded his arms. "It is a simple story. I have been a heathen and grown old among the heathen, and I know how the heathen think. Once a preacher came to our village to explain to us that there was a God." He stopped and chuckled to himself before continuing. "We asked him, 'Do you think us so ignorant that we do not know that? Go back to where you came from!'

"And so he left us. Then another white man came, and he said, 'You must not steal. You must not lie. You must not get drunk.' And we said to him. 'You fool. Don't you think we know that already? Learn the lessons you preach yourself before you try to convince us with your teaching. For who are bigger thieves, or who lies more often, or who is more frequently drunk than your own white people?'

"And that preacher went away too. But then Christian Henry came to visit our village."

"What was different about him?" Ludwig asked, leaning closer to Tschoop.

"Ah, he spoke as one who knew. He told us of a mighty one, the Lord of earth and sky, who left His glory in the heavens to give His life for all men. He told us that this God loves poor Indian sinners and longs to gain our love and to be our Savior and take us to His Father's home above."

"So that is what convinced you?" Ludwig asked.

"That, and what he did next. He concluded his preaching by saying, 'Friends, I am weary with my journey, and I want to lay down my head, so please excuse me.' And with that he lay down beside our spears and arrows and immediately fell into a peaceful sleep. We looked at each other, and I whispered, 'This is new. Yes, we have heard glad tidings, and this sleeper here knows them to be true. Look, he knows he has a friend above, or why else would he sleep here with men of war all around him and the war whoop in his ear?'

"We watched him all night, and in the morning, we told him that he need not journey on, that we wanted him to stay and tell us more about the loving, dying one. And that is how I heard of Jesus and came to have fellowship with Him."

"How wonderful!" Ludwig exclaimed. "When our Savior's love and suffering are preached, He will draw all men to Himself. How many of you are Christians now?"

"There are thirty-one that I know of, and I am sure many more will follow," Tschoop answered.

"So you are the firstfruit from among the Indian tribes. We are going to send out many others to preach the gospel to all tribes. Perhaps some of your tribe will go with us to spread the word!"

The two men continued talking into the night, and Ludwig became more excited than ever about sending missionaries into Indian country. There was just one problem. Many of the nearby Indian tribes were hostile toward white people and would not allow them to pass through their land. Ludwig realized that the Moravians would have to get permission to move among the Indian tribes before they preached to them. On July 4, 1742, he, Benigna, Anna Nitschmann, who was now at Bethlehem, and ten other Moravians set out on horseback to find the village of Meniolagomeka, where Ludwig had been told the chiefs of the Six Nations Iroquois Confederation were gathered.

For Ludwig, who in Europe traveled mostly in a coach, it was exhilarating to be on horseback, riding through the American wilderness. The group wound their way up and over the Blue Mountains, stopping at small Indian villages along the way. Five days after setting out from Bethlehem, they reached Meniolagomeka.

The chiefs of the Iroquois Confederation were not at the village, however. It was then that Ludwig had a strong feeling that they should travel on to Tulpehocken, where Conrad Weiser, a well-known mediator and interpreter between Indians and whites, lived. Ludwig had met Conrad when he attended one of the synods. He was impressed with Conrad's understanding of how the Indians thought.

When the group reached Tulpehocken, they found Conrad and the Indian chiefs they had been searching for. Each chief was dressed in buckskin pants and moccasins, with a blanket draped across one of his shoulders, and wore a feather headdress. To Ludwig, the men looked both fierce and noble.

With Conrad's help, Ludwig and the Moravians began a long and fruitful conversation with the chiefs. At first the chiefs were reserved, but Ludwig spoke quietly, explaining how the Moravians meant them no harm and were not looking to take their natural resources or cause them any disturbance. Slowly Ludwig noticed that the chiefs' attitudes began to soften, and they began asking questions. By the end of their time together, the chiefs of the Six Nations promised Ludwig that the Moravians could pass through the land of the Iroquois Confederation as friends and not as strangers. They could also spend time in Iroquois territory if they so desired. To seal their agreement, the chiefs gave Ludwig a belt fashioned from 186 small beads made from polished shells called wampum, which many Indian tribes used for money or in ceremonies like this one.

Following the meeting with the chiefs of the Six Nations, Ludwig went on to Philadelphia before returning to Bethlehem. A letter from Erdmuth that bore sad news was waiting for him in Philadelphia. Two months before, their four-year-old son David had died and was buried in God's Acre at Herrnhaag. Of the twelve Zinzendorf children, only five were still alive.

There was also good news from home. In June 1742 Frederick the Great, the young king of Prussia, had come into possession of the territory of Silesia. Upon taking possession of this land, King Frederick had asked for Moravians to move there and set up settlements as they had done at Herrnhut and Herrnhaag. The king had also officially recognized the Moravian Church as an independent church with its own clergy. The only thing the church was forbidden to do was to try to attract new members out of the State Church. The Moravian Church was allowed, however, to accept new members from among those people who sought them out of their own free will. This kind of official recognition was a wonderful breakthrough.

Still more good news awaited Ludwig in a letter from George Schmidt, who sent a report of his work in South Africa among the Hottentots. Several months before, George had baptized his first Hottentot convert. Several others had been baptized a short time afterward, and now a small church had been established among them. However, George reported that the Dutch authorities in South Africa were not happy about what he was doing, and pressure was building to have him removed from the colony.

By the time Ludwig arrived back at Bethlehem, the plan to turn the place into a missionary-sending hub was coming along well. The system that was being put in place, which they called the Economy, was now generating enough money to support fifteen preachers and teachers. The rules of the Economy were strict. Members pledged to use all of their time, labor, and talents to build up the community.

The church owned all of the land, and the elders assigned each person a job. As they had been in Herrnhut, the people were divided into choirs. But unlike Herrnhut, members could not own their own business or make their own living. Instead, everyone's daily needs were met through people working together. The community built their own houses and produced their own clothes and boots, even sawing their own lumber, spinning their own yarn, and weaving their own cloth. They also tilled the land and planted crops and vegetables. They raised sheep, cattle, and chickens to provide meat, milk, and eggs. They also made their own bread. Soon the system became so efficient that they produced much more than they needed for themselves. They took their surplus food and manufactured goods to the market, where the items fetched top prices. All of the extra money was used to send out and support the community's missionaries.

The people lived a strict and disciplined life. The Moravian elders knew that it was only for a time, but the need for missionaries among the immigrants and the Indians was so great that everyone agreed that it was worth the sacrifice. The community even made up a motto in Latin that expressed their commitment to one another: *In commune oramus, in commune laboramus, in commune patimur, in commune gaudeamus* (Together we pray, together we labor, together we suffer, together we rejoice).

At the same time that the Economy was being established at Bethlehem, George Whitefield's venture at nearby Nazareth had fallen on financial hard times, and the property was put up for sale. Seizing the opportunity, Ludwig and the Moravians bought the property and established a community there as well. Soon both the Bethlehem and Nazareth communities were working diligently to send out more and more missionaries among the Indians.

Ludwig himself made two more daring trips into Indian country. On the first trip, he traveled to Shekomeko in Dutchess County, New York, about twenty-five miles east of the Hudson River on the border with Connecticut. Benigna, Anna, and Conrad accompanied him on the journey. It took them a week on rough trails over the Blue Mountains, through New Jersey, and across the Hudson River to get there.

Shekomeko was where Christian Henry Rauch had established a small mission two and a half years before among the Mahican Indians. Ludwig spent eight days at Shekomeko, where he baptized new converts and established the first Indian congregation of the Moravian Church. He also spent some time planning for an extension of the mission there to begin evangelizing among the neighboring white population.

On the second trip, Ludwig spent six weeks traveling up the Wyoming Valley in Pennsylvania to meet with the Shawnee Indians to ask permission for Moravian missionaries to enter their territory and work among them. The Shawnees, however, rebuffed Ludwig's overtures, and Ludwig returned to Bethlehem, disappointed but not defeated by the experience.

In early 1743 Ludwig felt that it was time for him to return home to Europe. He had heard some disturbing rumors about what was going on among the Moravians in Germany, and he decided he needed to go and get to the bottom of these troubling reports.

Chapter 12

# The Sifting Time

Ludwig chartered a ship called the *James* in New York to take him and the group traveling with him to London. On January 20, 1743, the *James* set sail under the command of Captain Nicholas Garrison. The crossing of the Atlantic Ocean went well until February 14, when the *James* ran into a fierce storm near the Scilly Islands off the southwesternmost point of England. Soon huge waves crashed against the ship, and the wind lashed at its rigging. As the ship creaked and pitched and rolled, everyone aboard became afraid—everyone, that is, except Ludwig. Prayer and hymn singing kept him calm and at peace throughout the whole ordeal.

When jagged, menacing rocks appeared on the storm-battered horizon, the captain informed Ludwig that the *James* would be smashed on them in a matter of hours. There was no way to avoid being carried to their deaths. Calmly Ludwig looked Captain Garrison in the eye. "This storm will be over in two hours," he announced with a certainty that seemed to leave the captain dumbfounded.

After two hours Ludwig informed his traveling companions to go out on deck and check on the weather. On deck they found Captain Garrison staring up at the sky. The ship was now bathed in sunlight that had broken through the thick blanket of billowing storm clouds above. The wind had died down and with it the mountainous seas.

After setting his ship back on course, Captain Garrison sought out Ludwig. "How could you so accurately forecast the storm's end?" he demanded. "I have never seen a storm end so suddenly. We were only minutes away from being cast onto the rocks!"

Ludwig smiled as he answered the captain. "For more than twenty years now I have enjoyed a trusting relationship with the Savior. So when I find myself in difficult or dangerous situations, the first thing I do is ask myself whether I am to blame. If I find something that the Savior is displeased with, I get down on my knees and ask His forgiveness. And when I do this, He forgives me, and at the same time I usually know how things will work out. Of course, if the Savior does not choose to tell me the outcome, I remain silent and conclude that it is better for me not to know. However, this was not one of those times. Instead the Savior assured me that the storm would pass and last only two more hours."

"It is a fantastic explanation you give, Count Zinzendorf!" Captain Garrison exclaimed. "Normally I would not be inclined to believe it. But I have observed you on this voyage—the Christianity you practice, the relationship you have with the Savior—and find I can easily accept your explanation."

Ludwig nodded. "We are often told to talk with God, but how wonderful it is to know that God talks back to us, don't you think?"

Three days later, on February 17, the *James* finally reached Dover, England.

From Dover Ludwig traveled to London, where he was amazed to learn of the growth of the Moravian Church in England during his time in Pennsylvania. Under the leadership of August Spangenberg, the church was particularly thriving in Yorkshire, in the north of the country. Ludwig decided to travel there and visit with his old friend August and see the work firsthand.

As he traveled north to Yorkshire, Ludwig, in keeping with the rumors he had heard while still in Pennsylvania, began to be concerned that the growth of the church in England had come at the expense of other denominations. The idea that the Moravians might be growing through members from other denominations coming to join them went against all the principles of unity and harmony among denominations that he strove for. When he finally arrived in Yorkshire, his mind was soon put at ease. He found that most of the people involved in the new Moravian work had not come from other established denominations, as he had feared.

After several weeks in England, Ludwig set out for Herrnhaag. Again sad news awaited him. On his return home he learned that yet another of his children, five-year-old Johanna, had died. She, too, had been buried in God's Acre at Herrnhaag. Now only four children remained: seventeen-year-old Benigna, who had accompanied him on the trip to Pennsylvania; sixteen-year-old Christian Renatus, who was acting as the pastor at Herrnhaag; seven-year-old Maria; and three-year-old Elisabeth.

Ludwig was glad to see Erdmuth again. Erdmuth had been away for eight months visiting church groups all over Europe and had not been present when both David and Johanna had died. Ludwig grew concerned for her, wondering how she would cope with grieving for two more of her children.

At Herrnhaag Ludwig found that the rumors he had heard while in Pennsylvania were true. The Moravian Church was trying to start new branches all across Europe by encouraging Christians to leave their own denominations and join with them. It was exactly the opposite of what he had hoped for. Ludwig wanted to see the Moravians help to bring unity among churches, not compete with them. He called a synod and told the elders of the Moravian Church what he thought of their expansion plans. Meekly the leaders apologized for their selfishness and pledged to follow Ludwig's vision for uniting Christians of all denominations.

In an attempt to explain to the people at Herrnhaag what being a true Christian really was, Ludwig found things beginning to go terribly wrong. He wanted to find simple words to talk about the work of the Holy Spirit and how the Spirit stirred the hearts of people from all denominations to love one another and work together. Since most Christians understood that God was their Father and Jesus their brother, in an effort to help them understand the work of the Spirit, Ludwig preached a series of sermons on how the Holy Spirit was their mother. This was very confusing for many at Herrnhaag, but they listened dutifully.

Next, Ludwig and his son, Christian Renatus, started preaching on the wounds of Christ as He hung on the cross. They got more and more poetic in their words, until they were telling the community that they were little "splinters in the cross" or "suckers of the Holy Blood of Christ." The community added its own twist to this teaching, and soon the church services were becoming quite strange.

Not long after this, Ludwig decided to invite the most pious of his followers to join the "Order of Little Fools." The basic idea was a good one, based upon Jesus' words, "Unless you become as little children, you shall not enter the kingdom of God." However, the new order did not truly follow Jesus' teaching. Christians at Herrnhaag began trying to "prove" how childlike they were. Usually this amounted to not doing any work and instead singing and playing all day long. The members of the order threw themselves huge parties, all the while trying to imitate little children. They also began to look down on missionaries as people who did not understand the "play way."

While all this was happening, Ludwig did not notice that the community at Herrnhaag was getting dangerously off track, even though many people tried to warn him. Unconcerned, he often left Herrnhaag to visit other Moravians in need of his leadership.

In December 1743 Ludwig made a daring trip to Russia with Christian Renatus and a few others. Three Moravian missionaries on their way to set up a missionary work in Mongolia had been imprisoned at Saint Petersburg upon entering Russia. Following their imprisonment, Ludwig had sent an envoy to Russia to see what could be done about gaining their freedom. Regrettably the same fate had befallen the envoy. The entire group was arrested and thrown into jail with the three missionaries. At the same time, an edict had been issued in Russia banning the work of the Moravians in the province of Livonia, where their work had been growing rapidly. Ludwig set out in person to see what he could do about the situation.

On December 23 Ludwig arrived in Riga, the capital of Livonia, where he hoped to get formal permission to carry on to Saint Petersburg. To his surprise, instead of receiving formal permission to travel on, Ludwig and his traveling party were themselves arrested by the governor of the region and locked up in the citadel, Riga's military fort. Ludwig was astounded that someone of his social rank would be treated this way. He waited patiently for the governor to recognize the impropriety of what he had done and send him on to Saint Petersburg.

Three weeks passed before anything happened. However, what happened was not what Ludwig expected. Instead of granting Ludwig permission to carry on to Saint Petersburg, the governor was ordered to expel Ludwig and his band of Moravian travelers from Russian soil. Three days later, a contingent of soldiers escorted Ludwig back to the Prussian border. The imprisoned missionaries would spend three and a half more years in jail before being released.

On his way home, Ludwig spent several months in Silesia helping the new Moravian congregations there get established.

When he arrived back at Herrnhaag, which by now was a large and thriving community of one thousand people, Ludwig received a report from Pennsylvania about the missionary work going on there. He read with interest and dismay how two young missionaries, David Zeisberger and Frederick Post, had established a mission station among the Indians in the Hudson River Valley. But white settlers in and around the area were very unhappy with their ministry. In their view, Indians were savages, and missionaries should not be trying to convert them to Christianity. Finally, in response to the settlers' complaints, the two missionaries were arrested, transported to New York City, and thrown into jail, where they stayed for seven weeks until the governor of Pennsylvania interceded on their behalf and secured their release.

News continued to flow in from other parts of the world, giving the twenty-four-hour prayer meeting plenty to focus on. The following year, 1745, good news came from Greenland. Johann Beck, a Moravian missionary there, told Ludwig how the work among the Eskimos was growing. In fact, it was growing so fast that the chapel the missionaries had built to hold services in was now too small. More than two hundred Eskimos were gathering regularly for services. Johann pleaded with Ludwig for a bigger chapel, and Ludwig arranged for a large frame church to be shipped north to Greenland in sections.

Ludwig and the Moravians were also delighted to hear that after many years of struggle, the mission in Surinam, South America, had finally taken root and was beginning to grow.

In Zeist, Holland, on May 20, 1746, Ludwig had the pleasure of officiating at his daughter Benigna's wedding. It was a joyous occasion as Benigna married Baron John von Watteville, the adopted son of Ludwig's old friend and fellow member of the Order of the Grain of Mustard Seed, Frederick von Watteville. Ludwig was particularly happy about the marriage because he had been the one to suggest it. John had been his personal assistant for several years, and Ludwig had seen qualities in him that he thought would make him a fine husband for Benigna. As a wedding present for the couple, Ludwig purchased the Gross-Hennersdorf estate from his aunt for them.

It was during the summer of 1747 that Ludwig received a surprise letter from a minister in the royal court in Dresden. The king of Saxony had made a trip to Herrnhut earlier in the year and was greatly impressed by what he saw there. The minister told Ludwig that the king began to question why he had banished Ludwig in the first place. After all, Ludwig had been responsible for the establishment of Herrnhut, and the people he saw there were making a real contribution to Saxony. The king of Saxony also noted that the king of Prussia had embraced the Moravians. The letter went on to say that the king had changed his mind and was going to issue a royal decree rescinding Ludwig's banishment. Ludwig was now welcome to return home!

Ludwig sat and read the letter several times, taking in its message. It was true. His banishment was over! He could scarcely believe it. Joy flooded through him. He could go home to his people at Herrnhut.

On October 11, 1747, the royal decree was issued, lifting Ludwig's banishment, but it went even further than that. The decree also invited Ludwig to establish additional Moravian settlements in Saxony. Tears ran down Ludwig's cheeks as he read a copy of the decree. What had been meant to harm him had turned out to be for the good of the Moravians.

Three days later Ludwig was back at Herrnhut. Excitement filled the air as people clamored to greet him. In truth he had made several secret trips to Herrnhut during his banishment from Saxony, but during those visits he could not openly flaunt his presence among the people for fear of being captured and imprisoned. This time, though, he went openly among the people. That afternoon two hundred people joined in a love feast to honor Ludwig. Afterward Ludwig preached to the group as he had done so many times in the past.

One of the highlights of Ludwig's return to Herrnhut was the opportunity to meet two Eskimo Christians who had returned with Matthäus Stach, one of the three original Moravian missionaries to go to Greenland. Ludwig thought back to the day Matthäus was commissioned as a missionary. Now fourteen years later, here was Matthäus with Eskimo converts, telling wonderful stories of the continued growth of the Moravian mission in Greenland.

Not long after his return to Herrnhut, Ludwig had the pleasure of commissioning Friedrich Hocker and Johannes Rüffer as missionaries. These two doctors were on their way to eastern Persia to find the Guebre people and establish a mission station among them. Ludwig had learned of this group of people from an American trader in Amsterdam. The trader had told him that the Guebres were descendants of the ancient Magi who came bearing gifts at Jesus' birth.

The year 1747 also brought good news from Pennsylvania. The communities in Nazareth and Bethlehem were flourishing. The Economy, which Ludwig had helped put in place while in Pennsylvania, had led to the development of at least thirty-two industries that were providing for the needs of the community and the support of missionaries. Ludwig also learned that a young woman named Susanne Kaske was preparing to go to Berbice (Guyana) to establish a mission among the Indians there. Susanne would be the first American-born missionary to leave the shores of North America.

The year 1747 brought some bad news as well. Count Henry Reuss died. Henry was Erdmuth's brother and Ludwig's brother-in-law. He had been a great help to Ludwig and the Moravians over the years.

Finally, in December 1748, while Ludwig was making a trip to England with a group of "pilgrims," his attention was brought back to the community at Herrnhaag. One of the men traveling to England with Ludwig was Karl von Peistel, a retired soldier who had become a well-respected leader at Herrnhut. Over the past few years, many people, including Erdmuth, Christian David, and John von Watteville, had tried to warn Ludwig about the excesses that were occurring at Herrnhaag. But always Ludwig had been unwilling to listen, saying that if the church was going too far in any one direction, given enough time it would come back to center. Now, aboard ship, Ludwig and Karl spent many hours talking. Karl told Ludwig how he and many others had been attracted to the Moravians because of their quiet, orderly lives. But the community at Herrnhaag was now just the opposite, and it saddened him to see the Moravians being laughed at because of their new ways of worship.

By the time he arrived in Dover, England, Ludwig could see the error of his ways. He was the head of the Unity of the Brethren, and he had allowed them, even encouraged them, to become unbalanced in their beliefs. He was sorry for what he had done and set about correcting it immediately. He wrote a stern letter to all of the Moravian congregations, telling them to return to their central call to live orderly lives, live in unity, and send out missionaries. He also wrote to his son, Christian Renatus, ordering him to step down from his position as pastor at Herrnhaag and come to London immediately. Ludwig wrote to David Nitschmann and Leonard Dober, asking them both to return to Germany to help get the community back on the right path.

These measures worked, and within a year the communities were back working hard, praying hard, and supporting those who went out to declare the gospel. This difficult period they had been through became known as the Sifting Time, after Luke 22:31–32, where Jesus said to Peter, "Simon, Simon, behold, Satan hath desired to have you, that he may sift you as wheat: But I have prayed for thee, that thy faith fail not: and when thou art converted, strengthen thy brethren."

Meanwhile, Ludwig had work to do in England. He decided to move his headquarters there while he fought for the rights of the Moravians in the American colonies. These were the rights to give an affirmation instead of taking an oath and to be exempt from joining the military. The Quakers, who also did not believe in oath taking or fighting, already had these rights, and Ludwig met with Thomas Penn and General James Oglethorpe, the former governor of Georgia, to work out a way to gain those same rights for his communities.

It was an uphill battle. Many members of Parliament did not take kindly to the idea of a German nobleman coming to their land and demanding rights for his people in their American colonies.

Thankfully, not every leader in England thought this way. During this time in London, Lord Granville approached Ludwig and offered to sell to the Moravians, at a bargain price, one hundred thousand acres of land in North Carolina. Of course Ludwig was delighted with the offer, and negotiations were begun in earnest to see whether a deal for the purchase of the land could be worked out.

With the help of Thomas Penn and James Oglethorpe, Ludwig was able to present a good case for why the Moravians should be granted the same rights as the Quakers. He argued that instead of being forced to do military service or threatened with jail for refusing to take oaths, the Moravians should be given encouragement because they made such good citizens. They worked hard, were honest and law abiding, and kept peace with the Indians. They also spent a lot of money building their communities and offered services that were not available anywhere else.

A bill was drawn up based on Ludwig's arguments and introduced into the English parliament.

Most of the opposition to the bill took the form of quoting rumors and stories about the sifting time, and Ludwig had to go to great lengths to show that this period of their community life was over and that they had returned to their stable roots. Eventually, on May 12, 1749, the British parliament passed the bill allowing the Moravians freedom from oath taking and from military service. The bill was titled *The Recognition of the Unitas Fratrum as an Old Episcopal Church by the Parliament of Great Britain, 1749.*

Ludwig was greatly pleased by this new recognition for the Moravians, and he looked forward to a time when they would spread across the New World. What he did not predict was that they would get a huge push in this from a very unexpected source.

Chapter 13

# To the Four Corners of the World

In October 1749 Count Casimir of Büdingen died and was succeeded by his son Gustav Frederick. Unlike his father, Gustav Frederick was not friendly toward the Moravians at Herrnhaag, and his dislike of them had grown following the excesses of the sifting time. As a result, Gustav Frederick decided to assert his new position over the Moravians at Herrnhaag. He demanded that the residents of Herrnhaag renounce their allegiance to the Moravian Church and to Ludwig and instead swear an oath of allegiance to him. If they failed to do this, he warned them, he would terminate the contract that allowed the Moravians to live on his land, and the residents of Herrnhaag would be forced to abandon their community.

Ludwig was stunned when news of this turn of events reached him in London. He supposed that Gustav Frederick assumed that he could bully the community at Herrnhaag into swearing allegiance to him, but Ludwig knew that the Moravians would not bow to him, even if it meant leaving their buildings and crops behind. And that is exactly what happened. All the residents of Herrnhaag declared that they were ready to pack up and abandon the community they had built if Gustav Frederick would not retract his demands. The new count refused to back down, and so the Moravians looked around for new places to live.

Within a few days a group of Moravians from Herrnhaag set sail for Pennsylvania. Before the year was over, five hundred people had left Herrnhaag, moving to other Moravian communities throughout Europe and various mission locations around the globe.

While Ludwig could see the benefit of the residents of Herrnhaag dispersing this way to the four corners of the world, he chastised himself for allowing the community to get so out of balance during the sifting time. Had he paid more attention and listened to those who tried to warn him of the excesses they saw, perhaps Herrnhaag could have been saved. But he had not listened until it was too late. All he could do was learn from his mistake and help the Moravians from Herrnhaag find other places to live.

Around this time another letter reached Ludwig in London. This letter told about Friedrich Hocker's arrival at Herrnhut on February 8, 1750. Friedrich was one of the two doctors Ludwig had commissioned to go as missionaries to the Guebres in Persia. Regrettably, the venture had not gone well for the two men. Along the way to the Guebres, they had twice been attacked and robbed by Kurdish bandits. During the second attack, Friedrich had been seriously wounded and almost died. Starving and nearly naked, the two men stumbled their way to Isfahan, where the British consul took them in and helped them. The consul also told them that most of the Guebre people had been massacred and that the few who had survived the massacre had been exiled. Unable to go on, the two missionaries decided to turn back to Herrnhut. On their return journey they were once again attacked and robbed by bandits. This time Johannes Rüffer was killed in the attack. Friedrich buried his companion along the way and continued to Herrnhut.

The letter saddened Ludwig. He'd had high hopes for the mission to Persia, but it was not to be at this time.

During 1751 Ludwig also learned that Herrnhut had lost one of its founders. Christian David had died at the age of sixty-one. Tears streamed down Ludwig's cheeks as he received the news. Ludwig thought back to the day in 1722 when he had first met Christian David, who had made such an impact on him with his enthusiasm and his drive. It was that enthusiasm and drive that had allowed Christian David to tirelessly lead Moravians from persecution to religious freedom at Herrnhut. In the process, Christian David had succeeded in transplanting the hidden seed of the ancient Unitas Fratrum from Moravia to a place where it could take root and grow and flourish once more. Ludwig would miss his old friend.

Despite the harrowing stories, such as Friedrich Hocker's, a growing stream of Moravians offered to go out as missionaries. In 1752, a group of Moravian missionaries set sail on the *Hope* from England, bound for the Labrador coast of northeastern Canada, where they planned to establish mission stations and work among the Eskimos of that region. Upon arrival on the Labrador coast, the first four missionaries went ashore and prepared to build a house at a place they named Hopedale.

After letting these missionaries off, the *Hope* sailed farther north up the coast to a place where five more missionaries and the captain went ashore. This is when things went terribly wrong. A group of Eskimos lured the men into an ambush and murdered them. The first mate of the *Hope,* who had stayed aboard ship, sailed back down the coast and evacuated the other four missionaries to Europe. Again Ludwig was greatly saddened that another mission endeavor had not gone as planned. But he accepted it as God's will.

The year 1752 was to bring Ludwig more sadness. Christian Renatus, who was still in London with his father, became ill with tuberculosis in late February and died on May 28 at the age of twenty-four. He was buried on the grounds of Lindsey House, the Moravian headquarters in Great Britain.

Fifty-two-year-old Ludwig grieved deeply for Christian Renatus, his only son to have survived to adulthood. During their time together in London, Ludwig had grown very close to his son. For many weeks afterward, tears would flow every time he thought of Christian Renatus. In a letter to the Moravian congregations concerning his son's death, Ludwig wrote, "I do not understand it…He [God] himself will make it clear to all hearts."

Erdmuth, who had been at Herrnhut when Christian Renatus had fallen ill, was in Zeist, Holland, on her way to London to visit him when news reached her of his death. She hurried across the English Channel and went straight to her son's grave, where she wept bitterly. Ludwig tried to comfort her, but he was weighed down with his own sadness. Although Christian Renatus was their ninth child to die, Erdmuth seemed unable to accept his death. Eventually she felt strong enough to return to Herrnhut, but she was never quite the same.

After mourning the death of Christian Renatus, Ludwig turned his attention back to the business of the Moravian Church, and in 1753 some good news reached him. A report on the mission work in the West Indies encouraged Ludwig greatly. The Moravians had now established mission works on Saint Croix and Saint John as well as Saint Thomas. And the work on Saint Thomas was flourishing. The church there had more than one thousand baptized members! And the missionaries were regularly sharing the gospel with over four thousand slaves who spoke more than sixty dialects. Ludwig smiled to himself as he read the report and thought back to the day he had dropped off Leonard Dober and David Nitschmann at the fork in the road at Bautzen. What a wonderful job they had done in laying the foundation for Moravian missions on the island. And while Leonard had had the privilege of reaping the firstfruit—Oly—there was now much fruit on the island.

Ludwig received more good news in 1753. Negotiations with Lord Granville were finally completed, and the Moravians purchased the 100,000-acre tract of land they had been offered in North Carolina. Ludwig named the land Wachovia, after his family's ancestral estate in Austria. Soon construction of a community modeled after Bethlehem, Pennsylvania, got under way. Ludwig named this new community Salem.

In February the following year, two plantation owners on the British island of Jamaica in the Caribbean asked Ludwig to appoint missionaries to come to the island and share the gospel with their slaves. Three Moravian missionaries were dispatched, and they arrived on Jamaica in October. The two planters fully supported the missionaries' work, giving them land on which to establish a mission station. Soon other planters wanted missionaries on their plantations as well, and more Moravian missionaries arrived on the island, among them Christian Henry Rauch, who came from Pennsylvania. Christian

Henry had been one of the first Moravian missionaries to evangelize among the North American Indians. Soon many slave converts were being baptized into the church on Jamaica.

By March 1755 Ludwig felt it was time to leave the work in England and return to Germany. He visited various Moravian congregations in Europe before meeting up with Erdmuth in Niesky. The two of them slipped quietly back into Herrnhut on June 2. Neither one wanted the usual fanfare that was associated with Ludwig's appearances. However, it was hard to escape the joy that the community felt when word got around that their leader had returned. Hymns and sonatas were played in his honor, and a huge love feast was held. Ludwig was quite overcome by the outpouring of love, and he broke down in tears several times. The people in the villages around Herrnhut were also excited to have Count Zinzendorf back among them.

Not long after Ludwig's arrival back at Herrnhut, Baron Huldenberg paid him a visit. The baron was the nobleman who had pushed hardest for Ludwig to be banished from Saxony nineteen years before.

Ludwig warmly welcomed Baron Huldenberg and the pastor from his estate, whom the baron had brought with him. He led them into the library, where they began the usual polite conversation. After a short while, Baron Huldenberg cleared his throat and looked nervously at Ludwig.

"I am here, Count Zinzendorf," the baron began, "to return a letter to you. As you may have heard, in

1751 my estate was burned to the ground. The only building that remained standing was my manor house, but it was badly damaged by the fire. I asked for everything possible to be salvaged from it, and among the charred remains, one of my servants found this piece of paper."

With that the baron reached very carefully into the leather pouch he was carrying and pulled out a scorched piece of paper. "It is dated 1735, and it is in your hand. I will read you what it says:

> It pains me that you are suspicious of me and my dear Herrnhut.... Had I the honor to meet you personally, you would see that I am no lover of disorder. If you knew Herrnhut, you might even wish that your village were like it.... Your father and I had such a satisfactory conversation together in Prague, that it distresses me to have a misunderstanding with his son.... I assure you further that I am faithfully yours, Zinzendorf.

"At the time," the baron went on, "I must confess that your letter only made me more angry with you and more determined to have you banished. But when I saw it again, after the fire, I was overcome with guilt for what I had done to you and your family. The truth is, I have heard nothing but good about your community, and you are a better man than I. I can only ask you to forgive me for the terrible wrong I have done and to count me as your friend and supporter of your work from now on."

Ludwig fought back tears as he replied. "I can assure you, Baron Huldenberg, that I have nothing but goodwill toward you. What you meant for evil the Lord turned to good. I submit in all things to God's will, and I believe my banishment served a greater purpose. As for your offer to support our work, we would like the opportunity to send Moravians to your estates to perform Christian work."

"Of course, of course," the baron responded with great enthusiasm. "I shall put my pastor at your disposal. May God expand and bless all that you do."

When Baron Huldenberg left, Ludwig hurried to find Erdmuth. The baron had given him the charred letter, and Ludwig read it aloud to Erdmuth and excitedly told her of the wonderful reconciliation that had taken place between the two of them.

True to his word, Baron Huldenberg became a staunch supporter of the Herrnhut community and sent his pastor along to the first Herrnhut Ministers Conference, which was held there the following year.

By now finances were a recurring problem for Ludwig and the Moravians. The church had two main sources of income. One was Ludwig's personal income from his various estates and investments, most of which he gave to the cause, and the other was the money that the communities raised by selling the produce and goods they had grown and made. However, the Moravians were always stretching their money to the limits so that they could establish more communities and send out more missionaries. The loss of Herrnhaag had cost thousands of pounds, and the Moravians in England had made some bad investments that left them deeply in debt.

It was time for an Economical Conference to see what could be done about the dire situation. It was a tense time; everyone seemed to have a different idea of what had gone wrong and how to fix it. Eventually five new measures were adopted. The first one separated the Zinzendorf property from the general property of the church. The second put the property of the church under the control of a College of Directors, made up of capable men who understood finances. The third measure committed the college to paying off at a regular rate all the debts the church had incurred, while the fourth measure asked all members of the church to pay a fixed amount each year into the general church fund. The final measure suggested that all those who paid into the general fund should have the right to send representatives to the church's General Conference.

These were bold new steps for men who were used to asking Ludwig what they should do, but everyone decided it was for the best. Ludwig was now fifty-five years old, and his health was failing. In fact, he considered the Economical Conference one of the ways he could tidy up the Moravians' affairs before he left them.

Just as the conference was finishing, terrible news arrived from America. A war was brewing there between England and France over the future of the colonies, and frequent skirmishes had taken place on the western frontier of Pennsylvania. The Moravians were loyal to the British because they were in a British colony, but most of the Indians in the region were fighting for the French. Occasionally Moravian settlements were targeted by the Indians. Several had been damaged, but nothing prepared the Moravians for what happened on the night of November 2.

Fifteen adults and one baby were stationed at the Gnadenhütten mission twenty miles northwest of Bethlehem. Hostile Indians surrounded the mission house that night and began shooting at the missionaries inside. Everyone inside the mission house fled upstairs. The Indians then set fire to the building, and the flames quickly spread to the second story. The Moravians on the second floor jumped for their lives, but bullets and tomahawks felled most of them as they hit the ground. Five people managed to escape the massacre, and they watched from the woods as the whole settlement, including the school, supply store, and church, went up in flames. Indian converts nearby came to their aid, but it was too late to save anything. The converts offered to take revenge on the Indians who had done the killing, but the Moravians reminded them that they were there to save lives, not take them.

Ludwig insisted on breaking the bleak news to the community at Herrnhut himself. Afterward he led the community in a prayer that none of the murderers would die before hearing and accepting the gospel. Fifteen men and women then stepped forward to take the place of the slain missionaries, and they were soon sent off to Pennsylvania.

The Moravians in Saxony were also directly touched by this conflict. What was the French and Indian War in North America spilled over into Europe and became known as the Seven Years War. In the course of the war, King Frederick II of Prussia invaded Saxony, and many Moravian settlements found themselves in the thick of the battle. A division of Prussian soldiers even made Berthelsdorf their headquarters.

Through it all, Ludwig went about his work. He continued to write hymns, especially hymns for children, which he compiled into a *Hymnbook for the Children*. He also busied himself writing books and papers for adults.

In 1756 Ludwig moved back into Bethel, the manor house he had built on his Berthelsdorf estate thirty-three years before. He set about transforming the place into what he called the Disciple House. Here, the various choirs took turns coming to spend time with Ludwig.

While this was going on, Ludwig began to notice that Erdmuth was not well. She had never really recovered from the death of Christian Renatus, and she slept a great deal of the time. She did not complain of any particular pain, but it was obvious that she had lost the will to live. Finally in June 1756 she was not able to get up at all. Five days later, in the early hours of June 18, she died.

Ludwig was devastated. He and Erdmuth had been married for thirty-four years and had shared the births of twelve babies and the deaths of nine of their offspring. They had been separated by church business for more months than they had been together, and now Ludwig began to question whether he had been the best possible husband to Erdmuth. Had he encouraged her enough? Had he thanked her for the tireless work she had done with the finances and the children? Or had he taken her for granted, expecting that she could shoulder the burden of the Moravian Church as well as he could? Was her early death the result of too much work? Such questions tormented Ludwig to the point that he was unable to attend Erdmuth's funeral. Instead, he stood watching from the second story of the manor house as she was laid to rest in God's Acre.

Nor did the questions go away once Erdmuth was buried. Ludwig continued to feel guilty and remorseful about the way he had expected so much of his wife. He became restless and traveled around a lot, but he no longer enjoyed talking to others. Instead he shut the door to the outside world whenever he could and sought solace in prayer.

A year went by, and finally Ludwig's son-in-law John approached him. John said that many of the elders had talked together and decided that Ludwig should get married again. Ludwig saw the wisdom in this. Since Erdmuth's death, he had been so alone. He considered marrying Anna Nitschmann, who had been a key leader among the Moravians for nearly as long as he had. Anna was forty-two years old, and he was fifty-six, but that was not the biggest problem. A much greater gulf than age separated them. No matter what else he had done, Ludwig was still a count, while Anna, no matter how wonderful her leadership skills, was in the eyes of German nobility nothing more than a peasant. Even in the most liberal of church circles it was unthinkable that a count would marry a peasant!

The more Ludwig thought about it, the more complicated the whole idea became. What would his aged mother say? Probably even harsher words than she had uttered to him when she learned of his ordination as a Lutheran pastor. And what about his titled cousins and siblings? Would marrying a peasant be the final insult to his family? Ludwig didn't know. All he knew was that he had to make a decision, and soon, as he was not getting any younger.

Chapter 14

# Destined to Bring Forth Fruit

On Monday, June 27, 1757, Count Nicolaus Ludwig von Zinzendorf married Anna Nitschmann in a private ceremony at the Disciple House at Berthelsdorf. Eleven people witnessed the marriage, and each of them agreed to keep it a secret until Ludwig felt the time was right to tell everyone.

At the same time, Ludwig abdicated his position as a count in the Holy Roman Empire and gave all of his titles and privileges to his nephew Ludwig. He hoped that this would stop some of the anger that his family might feel when they found out he had married a peasant. Besides, now that Christian Renatus was dead, Ludwig had no direct male heir to pass his titles and privileges on to when he died.

The newly married couple soon set off with a group of "pilgrims," including John and Benigna von Watteville and their daughter Elizabeth. They were headed for western Germany and Switzerland to visit Moravian congregations. Everywhere Ludwig went, he was asked to preach, sometimes in French, other times in German.

By the time fall rolled around, the weather had turned particularly cold, and Ludwig was not well. He stayed in Erdmuth's family home for a month until he felt well enough to continue traveling. The castle brought back many memories for Ludwig—the disabled carriage in the nearby river, coming to the castle for the first time, learning that his friend Henry was in love with his cousin Theodora, and asking Erdmuth's mother for Erdmuth's hand in marriage. Ludwig had plenty of time to think back on all these events as he recuperated. And as he reminisced, he was grateful for the faithful partner Erdmuth had been to him.

Ludwig and Anna returned to Herrnhut in January 1758 to a community where still only a few people knew they were married. Anna went back to her work in the single women's choir, and Ludwig to his meetings at the Disciple House. That summer the couple were off again, this time to Holland to encourage the Moravian work there. Ludwig visited Herrendyk and Zeist and encouraged both centers to concentrate on sending out missionaries.

Finally, in November, Ludwig sent a letter to all the Moravian congregations announcing his marriage to Anna Nitschmann and explaining why they had kept it a private matter for a year and a half. He waited to hear from his mother, but she was silent on the subject.

Ludwig and Anna arrived home from their trip on Christmas Eve, just in time for the wonderful song service.

Now that everyone knew that Ludwig and Anna were married, Anna moved into the Disciple House with her husband, and the two took up the role of pastoring the community at Herrnhut. They took particular delight in meeting with the children and teaching them new songs.

The year 1759 looked very promising. During the previous year Ludwig had approached the king of Denmark about establishing a Moravian colony in Iceland. He had received a letter back saying that the king would prefer that the Moravians start a work in the Nicobar Islands in the Indian Ocean, islands which the Danish East India Company had taken control of two years before. To do this, Ludwig negotiated permission for the Moravians to set up a base of operations in Tranquebar on the southeast coast of India. Now in 1759 fourteen men from the single men's choir were preparing to set out for India. Two of the men would undertake full-time mission work in the Nicobar Islands while the other twelve worked at their trades to raise the necessary money to support the endeavor.

The imminent departure of the missionaries for Tranquebar brought back memories of August

Franke's school in Halle in 1712, where Ludwig had met Bartholomaus Ziegenbalg. Bartholomaus had been a missionary in Tranquebar and was home on furlough, and the lunchtime that Ludwig spent talking to him had challenged him and ultimately changed the course of his life. Now forty-seven years later, the Moravians were going to establish their own mission colony in Tranquebar.

In November 1759 Ludwig became concerned for Anna, who was losing weight fast. Although Anna seldom complained, Ludwig could see that she was often in great pain. He sent for a doctor, but no one could say what was exactly wrong with her. Anna kept on working as much as she could while Ludwig continued to meet with the various choirs, lead services, and write the *Daily Watchwords and Doctrinal Texts* for the year 1761.

By April 1760, Ludwig had to face the fact that his new wife was dying of cancer. Anna could no longer get out of bed, and Ludwig visited her every day. On Sunday, May 4, Anna made a gallant effort and accompanied Ludwig to a service to hear the single sisters sing. During the service, however, Ludwig began to notice pains in his chest, and he found it difficult to breathe.

Suddenly, unbelievably, Ludwig also was seriously ill! He felt so sick that he wondered whether he might die before Anna. All of Herrnhut heard the news and were allowed to visit Ludwig with their choirs. Although Ludwig was surrounded with continuous rounds of hymn singing, prayers, and Bible readings, he continued to grow weaker.

On May 8 Ludwig looked around at the many members of the community who had gathered round him. His chest was tight, and his lungs gurgled when he breathed, but he made the effort to talk. He turned to Bishop David Nitschmann. Tears ran down his cheeks as he spoke.

"Did you suppose, in the beginning, that the Savior would do as much as we now really see among the various Moravian settlements, amongst the children of God of other denominations, and amongst the heathen? I only entreated Him for a few firstfruits of the latter, but there are now thousands of them. Nitschmann, what a formidable caravan from our church already stands around the Lamb!"

Later that night Ludwig called his daughters and his son-in-law to his side. He gave his daughters advice about the estates and various business dealings, and then he turned to his son-in-law, John.

"Now, my dear friend, I am going to the Savior. I am ready. I bow to His will. He is satisfied with me. If He does not want me here anymore, I am ready to go to Him. There is nothing to hinder me now."

John reached for Ludwig's hand and began to pray. "Lord, now let Your servant depart in peace. The Lord bless thee, and keep thee; the Lord make His face shine upon thee, and be gracious unto thee; the Lord lift up His countenance upon thee and give thee peace."

Ludwig lifted his head off his pillow and then lay back down again. His chest stopped heaving, and his eyes were fixed upward. Count Nicolaus

Ludwig von Zinzendorf was dead. It was 10:00 PM on Friday, May 9, 1760, seventeen days short of his sixtieth birthday.

The hundred or so people who had been standing watch at the Disciple House wept quietly when they heard of Ludwig's passing. John went into Anna's room to tell her that Ludwig had died. Anna nodded, as if she were expecting the news, and replied, "I have the happiest prospect of you all. I will soon be going to him."

The trombones, which played whenever there was a death at Herrnhut, sounded loud and clear the following morning. As tendrils of mist wafted through the surrounding forest, people recognized the death tune. Their only question was, had they lost the father of their community or the mother?

Soon enough the people found out that it was Ludwig who had gone from them. Ludwig's body was dressed in the white surplice that he, as a Lutheran pastor, had worn when he officiated at communion. Ludwig was lifted into a purple-lined coffin and lay in state in the drawing room. Thousands of people from all walks of life came to file past his body and say their final good-byes to a man who had somehow crossed all of the social lines of the day and become their friend. That night, several of the men carried Anna into the drawing room to say her last good-bye as well.

The community waited a week to bury Ludwig, giving some time for those from the other communities to gather for his funeral. Finally on the evening of May 15, the funeral procession wound its way to God's Acre. Leading the procession was a group of singing children dressed in white. Behind them came Ludwig's three surviving daughters, Benigna, Maria, and Elisabeth, along with John von Watteville, Bishop David Nitschmann, and Frederick von Watteville. Frederick proudly wore the ring of the Order of the Grain of Mustard Seed, which Ludwig had given to him over forty years before.

When the procession reached the grave site, members of the Herrnhut community, residents of nearby villages and towns, and visitors crowded around to hear David Nitschmann speak as the coffin was lowered into the ground beside Countess Erdmuth's grave. "With tears we sow this seed in the earth; but He, in His own good time, will bring it to life and will gather in His harvest with thanks and praise! Let all who wish for this say Amen."

Four thousand voices echoed "Amen."

Anna was too ill to attend the funeral, but she watched it, propped up at a window in the single women's dormitory. Seven days later, on May 22, she, too, died and was buried beside her husband. By then Ludwig's gravestone had been laid in place. It read:

> Here lie the remains of that unforgettable man of God, Nicolaus Ludwig Count and Lord of Zinzendorf and Pottendorf. Through God's grace and his own faithful and untiring service he became the honored Ordinary of the

Brethren's Unity, renewed in this eighteenth century. He was born at Dresden on May 26, 1700, and entered into the joy of his Lord on May 9, 1760. He was destined to bring forth fruit, fruit that should remain.

Epilogue

# The Work Goes On

While the death of Count Zinzendorf was a blow to the Moravian Church, it marked a new phase and not the end of the church's growth. Ludwig had acted as the general arbiter in the church, laying out the rules for the various communities and congregations and making most of the major decisions. Now with his passing, the church decided that it was time to take another look at the way it was structured. Over the next several years, key Moravian leaders met together to draft a constitution for the church and establish a framework of leadership and governance that would carry them into the future.

Nor did the death of Count Zinzendorf cause the Moravians to neglect the missionary endeavors that

Ludwig had been so pivotal in helping to establish. At the time of the count's death, the Moravians had sent out 226 missionaries and baptized over 3,000 converts. The church continued to send out missionaries to the mission field, expanding existing missions and establishing new mission locations.

The Moravian mission work on Saint Thomas, Saint Croix, and Saint John continued to grow and develop. In the first fifty years of their missionary work there, they baptized 8,833 adults and 2,974 children.

The work of the Moravian Church also spread to many other islands of the Caribbean, including Antigua, where between 1769 and 1792 the number of Moravian converts on the island grew from 14 to 7,400.

In Surinam the missionaries were caught in the fighting between Indians and slaves. Unable to subdue the rebellion that was occurring, the government eventually granted the slaves their freedom, and the fighting subsided. The Moravians then set up more mission centers and went back to working among the Indians and slaves alike. But even then the Moravian mission work struggled along through epidemics and food shortages. The missionaries were forced to close several of their bases of operation. Despite the difficulties, they refused to abandon their work in Surinam. Over time the missionaries' determination paid off, and many thousands of converts were added to the church there.

Three more mission communities were established among the Eskimos in Greenland as the work there continued to grow. And ten years after Count Zinzendorf's death, Moravians from Great Britain were successful in finally establishing four mission centers along the Labrador coast of Canada. However, it took many years of patient work by these missionaries before any of the natives responded to the gospel that the missionaries had come to share.

Mission work among the Indians of North America also continued. The French and Indian War had been a very difficult time for the Moravians living and working among the Indians. The French had tried to get as many Indian tribes as possible to go on the warpath against the English. The Moravians had found themselves caught in the middle, trying to keep themselves and the Indians in their mission communities out of harm's way. This had not always been possible, as demonstrated by the massacre of Moravian missionaries at Gnadenhütten, Pennsylvania, on November 24, 1754.

Eventually the war had come to an end, and hostilities had died down. The Moravians had then gone back to their work among the Indians, where one of the features of their work was their insistence on learning the language of the tribe they were working among and using that language for all of their teaching and preaching. As a result, a trust and rapport was established between the Moravians and the Indians.

David Zeisberger was one Moravian missionary who enjoyed a productive ministry to the Indians. After the French and Indian War, he established missions among the Indians on the western frontier, eventually establishing Schönbrunn (Beautiful Spring) on the Tuscarawas River in southeastern Ohio. A short while later, Gnadenhütten, named after the ill-fated mission station in Pennsylvania, was established ten miles farther south. Many Delaware Indians as well as Indians from other Moravian settlements migrated to these settlements. They cleared land, planted crops, and raised cattle. Schönbrunn and Gnadenhütten were thriving communities, filled with peaceable converts who had renounced many of their old practices and had vowed to never again go on the warpath.

Later, another war—the Revolutionary War—engulfed the communities. Schönbrunn and Gnadenhütten were located between the British military outpost in Detroit and the Americans in Pittsburgh. David and his fellow Moravian missionaries were viewed with suspicion by both sides. Each side suspected them of being spies for the other and of inciting the Indians to side with the enemy in the war. Of course, nothing could have been further from the truth. The Moravians and the members of their communities were pacifists and took a neutral stand in the war.

Eventually British soldiers arrived and forced the residents of Schönbrunn and Gnadenhütten to abandon their land and crops. The residents were then herded north to Sandusky, where they endured a harsh winter during which they nearly starved to death. From Sandusky, David and the Moravian missionaries with him were ordered to Detroit to be tried by the British as American spies. As spring approached, and with their missionaries gone, about 150 starving Indian converts sought and received permission to return temporarily to Gnadenhütten to glean what they could of their crops from the fields.

As the Indians gathered food from the field, ninety American volunteers under the command of Colonel David Williamson descended upon them. This group of American soldiers had been dispatched from Pittsburgh to avenge the death of a white farmer and his family, who were allegedly killed by Indians who spoke German. The Indians befriended the soldiers when they arrived and fed them, but the soldiers repaid this hospitality by brutally massacring the entire group the following morning, March 8, 1782. Of the 150 Indians, only two small boys managed to escape and report the horrific killings.

More than one hundred years after the atrocities at Gnadenhütten, President Theodore Roosevelt called the massacre a "deed of revolting brutality" and said, "even now a just man's blood boils in his veins at the remembrance."

The massacre at Gnadenhütten had a deep impact upon the work of all missionaries working among the Indians. The Moravians tried to pick up where they had left off at the end of the Revolutionary War, but the massacre had changed the attitude of many Indians. While a number of the converts drifted back to the Moravian communities, many Indians asked why they should accept the white man's religion. After all, look at what it had got them—bloodshed and heartache. From this time on, missionary work among the Indians of North America became a much more difficult task, as missionaries now had to overcome deep-rooted suspicion and resentment.

David Zeisberger continued his work among the Indians for twenty-five more years, but his work never attained the same momentum and vibrancy that it had before the events at Gnadenhütten.

Despite the setbacks, the work of David and the other Moravian missionaries living among the Indians of North America did have an impact, not only on the Indians but also on white people. Author James Fenimore Cooper, the first American novelist to achieve worldwide fame, spent much of his early life on the frontier in New York surrounded by Indians. There he also met many of the Moravian missionaries working among them, and he was greatly challenged by what he saw. The journals of David Zeisberger and several other Moravians provided the inspiration and source material for many of the stories in his Leatherstocking Tales series. And early Moravian convert Tschoop is recognized as the model for the character Chingachgook in Cooper's 1826 novel *The Last of the Mohicans.*

The missionary zeal of Count Zinzendorf reached far beyond the Moravians themselves. In many ways Ludwig's life influenced more Christians outside the Moravian church than those in it. John Wesley had visited Herrnhut to personally observe this vibrant community. And while he had some doctrinal differences with the Moravians, he introduced many of the Moravian practices into the Methodist Church, which he founded. And in 1792 at a small gathering of Baptist pastors in Kettering, England, William Carey, who was destined to be the first Baptist missionary, tossed copies of the Moravian magazine *Periodical Accounts* onto the table and declared, "See what the Moravians have done! Can't we Baptists at least attempt something in fealty [devotion] to the same Lord?"

The Moravians at Herrnhut continued to pray for missionaries around the globe. In fact, the twenty-four-hour prayer chain started in 1727 continued unbroken for over one hundred years.

Today, more than two hundred years after Ludwig's death, the spirit that Count Nicolaus Ludwig von Zinzendorf tried so hard to foster lives on, both in the Moravian Church and in the many other missionary organizations around the world. Count Zinzendorf sought only the firstfruits, but today, largely as a result of his vision and dedication, many millions more have been added to the unity of all believers.

# Bibliography


Hamilton, J. Taylor, and Kenneth G. Hamilton. *History of the Moravian Church: The Renewed Unitas Fratrum 1722–1957.* Bethlehem, PA: Moravian Church in America, 1967.

Hutton, J. E. *History of the Moravian Church.* London: Moravian Publication Office, 1909.

Langton, Edward. *History of the Moravian Church.* London: Allen & Unwin, 1956.

Lewis, A. J. *Zinzendorf: The Ecumenical Pioneer.* London: SCM Press, 1962.

Sawyer, Edwin A. *These Fifteen: Pioneers of the Moravian Church.* Bethlehem, PA: Comenius Press, 1963.

Weinlick, John R. *Count Zinzendorf: The Story of His Life and Leadership in the Renewed Moravian Church.* Bethlehem, PA: Moravian Church in America, 1989.

## About the Authors

Janet and Geoff Benge are a husband and wife writing team with thirty years of writing experience. Janet is a former elementary school teacher. Geoff holds a degree in history. Originally from New Zealand, the Benges spent ten years serving with Youth With A Mission. They have two daughters, Laura and Shannon, and an adopted son, Lito. They make their home in the Orlando, Florida, area.

# *Also from Janet and Geoff Benge…*

More adventure-filled biographies for ages 10 to 100!

**Christian Heroes: Then and Now**

*Gladys Aylward: The Adventure of a Lifetime* • 978-1-57658-019-6
*Nate Saint: On a Wing and a Prayer* • 978-1-57658-017-2
*Hudson Taylor: Deep in the Heart of China* • 978-1-57658-016-5
*Amy Carmichael: Rescuer of Precious Gems* • 978-1-57658-018-9
*Eric Liddell: Something Greater Than Gold* • 978-1-57658-137-7
*Corrie ten Boom: Keeper of the Angels' Den* • 978-1-57658-136-0
*William Carey: Obliged to Go* • 978-1-57658-147-6
*George Müller: Guardian of Bristol's Orphans* • 978-1-57658-145-2
*Jim Elliot: One Great Purpose* • 978-1-57658-146-9
*Mary Slessor: Forward into Calabar* • 978-1-57658-148-3
*David Livingstone: Africa's Trailblazer* • 978-1-57658-153-7
*Betty Greene: Wings to Serve* • 978-1-57658-152-0
*Adoniram Judson: Bound for Burma* • 978-1-57658-161-2
*Cameron Townsend: Good News in Every Language* • 978-1-57658-164-3
*Jonathan Goforth: An Open Door in China* • 978-1-57658-174-2
*Lottie Moon: Giving Her All for China* • 978-1-57658-188-9
*John Williams: Messenger of Peace* • 978-1-57658-256-5
*William Booth: Soup, Soap, and Salvation* • 978-1-57658-258-9
*Rowland Bingham: Into Africa's Interior* • 978-1-57658-282-4
*Ida Scudder: Healing Bodies, Touching Hearts* • 978-1-57658-285-5
*Wilfred Grenfell: Fisher of Men* • 978-1-57658-292-3
*Lillian Trasher: The Greatest Wonder in Egypt* • 978-1-57658-305-0
*Loren Cunningham: Into All the World* • 978-1-57658-199-5
*Florence Young: Mission Accomplished* • 978-1-57658-313-5
*Sundar Singh: Footprints Over the Mountains* • 978-1-57658-318-0
*C.T. Studd: No Retreat* • 978-1-57658-288-6
*Rachel Saint: A Star in the Jungle* • 978-1-57658-337-1
*Brother Andrew: God's Secret Agent* • 978-1-57658-355-5
*Clarence Jones: Mr. Radio* • 978-1-57658-343-2
*Count Zinzendorf: Firstfruit* • 978-1-57658-262-6
*John Wesley: The World His Parish* • 978-1-57658-382-1
*C. S. Lewis: Master Storyteller* • 978-1-57658-385-2
*David Bussau: Facing the World Head-on* • 978-1-57658-415-6
*Jacob DeShazer: Forgive Your Enemies* • 978-1-57658-475-0
*Isobel Kuhn: On the Roof of the World* • 978-1-57658-497-2
*Elisabeth Elliot: Joyful Surrender* • 978-1-57658-513-9
*D. L. Moody: Bringing Souls to Christ* • 978-1-57658-552-8
*Paul Brand: Helping Hands* • 978-1-57658-536-8
*Dietrich Bonhoeffer: In the Midst of Wickedness* • 978-1-57658-713-3
*Francis Asbury: Circuit Rider* • 978-1-57658-737-9
*Samuel Zwemer: The Burden of Arabia* • 978-1-57658-738-6

*Klaus-Dieter John: Hope in the Land of the Incas* • 978-1-57658-826-2
*Mildred Cable: Through the Jade Gate* • 978-1-57658-886-4
*John Flynn: Into the Never Never* • 978-1-57658-898-7
*Richard Wurmbrand: Love Your Enemies* • 978-1-57658-987-8
*Charles Mulli: We Are Family* • 978-1-57658-894-9
*John Newton: Change of Heart* • 978-1-57658-909-0
*Helen Roseveare: Mama Luka* • 978-1-57658-910-6
*Norman Grubb: Mission Builder* • 978-1-57658-915-1
*Albert Schweitzer* • 978-1-57658-961-8

## Heroes of History

*George Washington Carver: From Slave to Scientist* • 978-1-883002-78-7
*Abraham Lincoln: A New Birth of Freedom* • 978-1-883002-79-4
*Meriwether Lewis: Off the Edge of the Map* • 978-1-883002-80-0
*George Washington: True Patriot* • 978-1-883002-81-7
*William Penn: Liberty and Justice for All* • 978-1-883002-82-4
*Harriet Tubman: Freedombound* • 978-1-883002-90-9
*John Adams: Independence Forever* • 978-1-883002-50-3
*Clara Barton: Courage under Fire* • 978-1-883002-51-0
*Daniel Boone: Frontiersman* • 978-1-932096-09-5
*Theodore Roosevelt: An American Original* • 978-1-932096-10-1
*Douglas MacArthur: What Greater Honor* • 978-1-932096-15-6
*Benjamin Franklin: Live Wire* • 978-1-932096-14-9
*Christopher Columbus: Across the Ocean Sea* • 978-1-932096-23-1
*Laura Ingalls Wilder: A Storybook Life* • 978-1-932096-32-3
*Orville Wright: The Flyer* • 978-1-932096-34-7
*Captain John Smith: A Foothold in the New World* • 978-1-932096-36-1
*Thomas Edison: Inspiration and Hard Work* • 978-1-932096-37-8
*Alan Shepard: Higher and Faster* • 978-1-932096-41-5
*Ronald Reagan: Destiny at His Side* • 978-1-932096-65-1
*Davy Crockett: Ever Westward* • 978-1-932096-67-5
*Milton Hershey: More Than Chocolate* • 978-1-932096-82-8
*Billy Graham: America's Pastor* • 978-1-62486-024-9
*Ben Carson: A Chance at Life* • 978-1-62486-034-8
*Louis Zamperini: Redemption* • 978-1-62486-049-2
*Elizabeth Fry: Angel of Newgate* • 978-1-62486-064-5
*William Wilberforce: Take Up the Fight* • 978-1-62486-057-7
*William Bradford: Plymouth's Rock* • 978-1-62486-092-8
*Ernest Shackleton: Going South* • 978-1-62486-093-5
*Benjamin Rush: The Common Good* • 978-1-62486-123-9
*Dwight Eisenhower: Supreme Commander* • 978-1-62486-142-0
*Frederick Douglass: The Right to Dignity* • 978-1-62486-151-2